Early Pentecostals on
Nonviolence and Social Justice

Early Pentecostals on Nonviolence and Social Justice

A Reader

EDITED BY

Brian K. Pipkin

AND

Jay Beaman

FOREWORD BY

Ronald J. Sider

☙PICKWICK *Publications* • Eugene, Oregon

EARLY PENTECOSTALS ON NONVIOLENCE AND SOCIAL JUSTICE
A Reader

Pentecostals, Peacemaking, and Social Justice 10

Copyright © 2016 Wipf and Stock Publishers. All rights reserved. Except for brief quotations in critical publications or reviews, no part of this book may be reproduced in any manner without prior written permission from the publisher. Write: Permissions, Wipf and Stock Publishers, 199 W. 8th Ave., Suite 3, Eugene, OR 97401.

Pickwick Publications
An Imprint of Wipf and Stock Publishers
199 W. 8th Ave., Suite 3
Eugene, OR 97401

www.wipfandstock.com

PAPERBACK ISBN: 978-1-4982-7891-1
HARDCOVER ISBN: 978-1-4982-7893-5
EBOOK ISBN: 978-1-4982-7892-8

Cataloguing-in-Publication data:

Names: Pipkin, Brian J., editor. | Beaman, Jay, editor. | Sider, Ronald J., foreword.

Title: Early pentecostals on nonviolence and social justice : a reader / edited by Brian J. Pipkin and Jay Beaman ; foreword by Ronald J. Sider.

Description: Eugene, OR : Pickwick Publications, 2016. | Series: Pentecostals, Peacemaking, and Social Justice 10. | Includes bibliographical references and index.

ISBN 978-1-4982-7891-1 (paperback) | ISBN 978-1-4982-7893-5 (hardback) | ISBN 978-1-4982-7892-8 (ebook)

Subjects: Pentecostal churches—Doctrines. | Peace—Religious aspects—Pentecostal churches.

CLASSIFICATION: LCC BX8762.Z5 E27 2016 (PRINT) | BX8762.Z5 E27 (EBOOK)

Manufactured in the U.S.A.   11/03/16

To Brenna, Connor, and Brogan
Never stop questioning

Contents

Foreword by Ronald J. Sider | xi
Preface by Brian K. Pipkin | xiii
Introduction by Jay Beaman | xv
About the Authors | xix

1. "The Gold, White and Blue" | 1
   Frederick A. Graves

2. "Imminent Events in the United States" | 2
   Charles Fox Parham

3. Should a Christian Fight? | 6
   Samuel Booth-Clibborn

4. "Victory" | 17
   Lillian Thistlethwaite

5. "War! War! War!" | 19
   Charles Fox Parham

6. Blood Against Blood | 20
   Arthur Sydney Booth-Clibborn

7. "The Character of the Church" | 27
   William J. Seymour

8. "Should Christians Go to War?" | 28
   William Burt McCafferty

9. "The Present Situation" | 31
   Ambrose Jessup Tomlinson

Contents

10 "The European War" | 34
Frank Bartleman

11 "Present Day Conditions" | 39
Frank Bartleman

12 "Christian Preparedness" | 43
Frank Bartleman

13 "Is Christian Civilization Breaking Down?" | 47
Frank Bartleman

14 "Pentecostal Saints Opposed to War" | 50
The Weekly Evangel

15 "What Will the Harvest Be?" | 51
Frank Bartleman

16 "Our Heavenly Citizenship" | 57
Stanley Frodsham

17 "In the Last Days" | 60
Frank Bartleman

18 "The World War" | 64
Frank Bartleman

19 "Loyalty and Perseverance" | 67
Ambrose Jessup Tomlinson

20 "The Christian and War: Is It Too Late?" [Part 1] | 69
Samuel Booth-Clibborn

21 "The Christian and War: Christ Cleansing the Temple" [Part 2] | 72
Samuel Booth-Clibborn

22 "The Spirit of the Age" | 76
H. Musgrave Reade

23 "The Awful World War" | 82
Ambrose Jessup Tomlinson

24 "The Awful War Seems Near" | 86
Ambrose Jessup Tomlinson

25 "War Notice" | 90
Ambrose Jessup Tomlinson

Contents

26 "The Pentecostal Movement and the Conscription Law" | 93
The Weekly Evangel

27 [Members Seeking Conscientious Objection] | 95
C. H. Mason

28 "Days of Perplexity" | 96
Ambrose Jessup Tomlinson

29 "The Patriotic Harlot" | 101
Elbert Carlton Backus

30 "Christian Citizenship" | 105
Frank Bartleman

31 "War and the Christian" | 112
Frank Bartleman

32 "From the Pentecostal Viewpoint" | 126
Stanley Frodsham

33 "War, the Bible, and the Christian" [Part 1] | 132
Donald Gee

34 "War, the Bible, and the Christian" [Part 2] | 137
Donald Gee

35 "War Behind the Smoke Screen" | 142
The Pentecostal Evangel

36 "The Way to Disarm Is to DISARM" | 144
Aimee Semple McPherson

37 "The Pulse of a Dying World" | 147
William Booth-Clibborn

38 Is War Christian? | 152
Frederic B. Phillips

39 "Conscientious Objection" | 158
Donald Gee

Bibliography | 163
Subject Index | 165
Scripture Index | 169

Foreword

Ronald J. Sider

PENTECOSTALISM IS THE MOST rapidly growing movement in global Christianity. And it is the largest segment of Protestantism. Unfortunately, in many people's minds, Pentecostals are associated with an otherworldly spirituality with little concern for injustice today; or with a "Gospel of Wealth" theology that ignores today's unjust economic structures; or with an uncritical nationalism that fails to critique war and violence.

But in the last couple decades, scholars have demonstrated that early Pentecostals were often pacifists, critics of unfair economic systems, and advocates of racial and gender equality. One thinks, for example, of Jay Beaman's landmark work, *Pentecostal Pacifism* (1989), that established the groundwork for many subsequent studies on Pentecostal nonviolence, as well as documenting the pacifist orientation of many Pentecostal denominations including the Assemblies of God. Another illustration would be *Pentecostal and Holiness Statements on War and Peace* by the authors of this volume. Although not every scholar has fully agreed, this discovery of widespread opposition to war and injustice represents a large shift in our understanding of early Pentecostalism.

This book provides a major new contribution to this rediscovery. It offers an amazing collection of the actual published statements of some of the most influential early Pentecostal leaders. In these pages, we see them vigorously opposing war and denouncing economic, racial, and gender injustice. We hear Aimee Semple McPherson (founder of the influential Pentecostal denomination, The Foursquare Church) promoting gender equality, opposing capital punishment, and advocating peace. We listen to Ambrose Jessup Tomlinson (an early General Overseer of the large Pentecostal Church of God, Cleveland, Tennessee) denouncing war. We hear the words of Charles H. Mason (co-founder of the Church of God in Christ,

Foreword

the largest African-American Pentecostal denomination) who was monitored by the FBI for his strong pacifist and interracial views. And we read the statements of William J. Seymour (pastor of the Azusa Street Mission in Los Angeles where the US Pentecostal movement began in 1906) who vigorously supported interracial worship and gender equality. These are just a few of the most influential earliest leaders of Pentecostalism that this book enables the contemporary person to listen to in their own words.

Educated Christians, church leaders, and scholars will all profit from this significant new book.

Ronald J. Sider

Distinguished Professor of Theology, Holistic Ministry, and Public Policy
Palmer Theological Seminary of Eastern University.

Preface
Brian K. Pipkin

PENTECOSTAL PACIFISM IS NOT dead. It is marginal and on life support, but not extinct. For some, this radical and often forgotten legacy is embarrassing and consequently brushed off as haphazard and schismatic. In a time when many Pentecostal denominations have collectively marginalized their pacifist history, and because pacifism has been all but eliminated from Sunday sermon discourse, people are looking to their religious forbearers found within this book for guidance.

We do not attempt to circle the wagon. Other seminal works like *Pentecostal Pacifism* (1989/2009), *Peace to War* (2009), and *Pentecostal and Holiness Statements on War and Peace* (2013) have already provided a comprehensive summation of the seriousness to which Pentecostals engaged pacifist rhetoric/action. The uniqueness of this book, however, is providing a commentary-free, first-hand, primary-source account of Pentecostal nonviolence laid bare.

This book, composed of thirty-nine articles written by seventeen authors from 1901–1940, took two years to complete. We thoughtfully selected articles we think showcase the greatest contributions made by first-generation Pentecostals. Our goal is to put before you some significant proponents of early Pentecostal nonviolence. This motley crew of voices, we believe, showcases the most creative arguments on the early story of Pentecostal nonviolence. Not all Pentecostal pacifists are mentioned. Many did not have the opportunity to formally vocalize their protest of war within their denominational publications given that peace-talk was stigmatized and criminalized during wartime.

These writings, once accessible only by academics, are now available to everyone. This book is a testament to the historical richness and theological depth of Pentecostal nonviolence. In some sense, this is an attempt to engage with the unconvinced—individuals and organizations that have dismissed this topic as unimportant or embarrassing and to counterbalance revisionist histories that caricature Pentecostal pacifism as an accident, an afterthought, haphazard, and schismatic.

The good news is that WWII did not completely extinguish all Pentecostal pacifists. The tradition continues. Today some of them are active in Pentecostals and Charismatics for Peace and Justice, a multicultural, gender-inclusive, and ecumenical network that helps enable Jesus-shaped Spirit-empowered peacemaking with justice (www.pcpj.org). This group is a successor of Pentecostalism's early peace tradition. They are present-day Tomlinsons and Bartlemans of this book.

It is our hope that these writings will help you think independently, critically, and suspiciously, and to challenge preconceived ideas of violence as redemptive, necessary, and good. The goal is not agreement with the themes presented in this book. Our goal is to let these forgotten voices retell their story to a new generation facing the same violence, economic turmoil, colonialism, racism, and stereotypes they faced many years ago.

Introduction

Jay Beaman

THE PENTECOSTAL WRITERS, LEADERS, and pastors presented in this book had one goal: to transform their culture from violence, nationalism, and racism to one of nonviolence and justice. To do so, they fought, but fought nonviolently, believing their weapons were spiritual, not carnal. In many of these articles and sermons you see evidence of the arguments in which they were engaged, often repeating the arguments of the other side. These early Pentecostals were in a struggle to be countercultural and nonconformist. Their aim was not only to promote the work of the Spirit in healing and holiness, but also in renewing the world. They believed prophetic work was a constant battle with rulers, Wall Street economics, governments, capitalism, corporations, nationalisms, religions, and all systems of concentrated power.

Today we live in a time of dramatic displacement of people around the world. Many from the Middle East are being displaced to Europe at great cost and risk. Europe and the US are asking questions about what is society and what is citizenship. With the great displacements that occurred after the Great War, the meaning of citizenship was debated in the US Some placed tests of loyalty upon citizenship. During the 1920s through the 1940s, immigrants seeking citizenship in the US were asked if they were willing to bear arms in defense of their newly chosen country. With what allegiance would Pentecostals be willing to swear an oath? It was not a philosophical question. Many of the articles explore this question from a theological point of view. William Booth-Clibborn, Pentecostal pastor in Portland, Oregon, as an immigrant, was sensitive to loyalty tests for immigrants. His brother, Samuel, was under surveillance by federal authorities during the Great War for conscientious objection and writings against warfare. His book was deemed unsuitable for mailing under the Espionage Act of 1918.

Introduction

William criticized the US Supreme Court ruling that failed to strike such narrow loyalty tests for citizenship. He had lived in Switzerland, England, Canada, and the US Like other Pentecostals writing in this volume, he held citizenship in any particular country lightly and held tightly to citizenship under the rule of God. At the time, a number of Pentecostals were on a federal list of conscientious objectors seeking citizenship and were being opposed by the US Department of Defense.

To read these articles, we are reminded that old time "Pentecost," as the movement was referenced, was prophecy. Many of the leaders were not so much administrators as they were prophets. Listen to some of the titles: "Immanent events in the United States" (Parham), "Present Day Conditions" (Bartleman), "The Present Situation" (Tomlinson), "The Spirit of the Age" (Reade), "What Will the Harvest Be?" (Bartleman), "In the Last Days" (Bartleman); all of them reading the newspapers and the events of the day as ominous and filled with meaning and portent. But, prophecy was not just prediction, it was a call to action and a challenge to the current line of action. Humanly speaking, Bartleman was lucky. While he was correct that "spies haunted every meeting," sometimes the right hand of the beast did not know what the left hand was doing. However, there were times when the authorities were on the lookout for him. Leaders of the Church of God in Christ, Assemblies of God, Church of God, and others were visited, statements taken, and monitors put in place. Consequently, the leadership of the Assemblies of God tried to distance themselves from their earlier promotion of Bartleman's articles and tracts. The truth was that many people, Pentecostals among them, were being jailed and imprisoned for lesser acts and statements than these folks were making.

It is important to note the timing of these articles. Many were in the lead-up to American entry to the Great War, before April 1917, reflecting the experiences of Pentecostals in England and Europe at the start of the conflict. But even with the Assemblies of God pushing back against Bartleman after being visited by the FBI, after WWI and in the lead-up to WWII, a variety of Pentecostals reprised their old position, strengthening it, and countering then-contemporary challenges.

These authors of articles, sermons, and book excerpts show some patterns. They are arguing ultimate values. They do not see peace and justice work as optional add-ons to their faith. Pentecostals saw peace and justice as central to their faith. It was grounded in the Bible, in the teachings of Jesus and the apostles, the teaching and example of the early church, the centrality of love, the new creation, forgiveness and reconciliation, and the worldwide community of faith. It was theological. And, it made them see their relationship to the nation state in a different light. It was also sociological. It made them see their relationship to the economy in different terms. They were critical of capitalism and wealth. They saw a willingness to send people to war and a willingness to go to war as participating in idolatry to wealth and power and a destruction of all of creation. They saw the conflicts in cosmological and prophetic terms. The Great War exhibited the work of Anti-Christ in its allegiances and destruction of humanity. At its core, warfare called into question human pretentions and the very idea of progress so central to the Enlightenment and modernity.

These leaders were also pragmatic. They organized, taught, and led their followers into conscientious objection to war. From Charles H. Mason (Church of God in Christ), to A. J. Tomlinson (Church of God), to Stanley Frodsham and Donald Gee (Assemblies of God); these leaders talked about the pragmatic decisions that would have to be made as their membership was drafted and had to make concrete decisions as to exactly where their conscience was engaged.

Of course, these documents must be seen in light of their times. With the global reach of the US military, the ascendency of capitalism and technology, perhaps, contrary to these early Pentecostal leaders we have indeed reached a golden age of peace, prosperity, and racial justice. What, you might ask, could we learn from century-old documents? What of a Booth-Clibborn decrying the 2 percent of wealthy who destroy the lives of the 98 percent poor? When one serious candidate for president (Donald Trump) calls for a wall at our southern border and the exclusion of Muslims from the US, and the call from the streets is that black lives matter, what can we learn from the early Pentecostal calls for racial justice and justice in our immigration policy?

About the Authors[1]

Elbert Carlton Backus was formerly a Methodist lay preacher, but removed from the ministerial rolls. By 1918, he transitioned to the Pentecostal faith, loosely called Holiness Mission or Holy Roller. It is possible that in transition from Methodist to Pentecostal he had espoused a form of socialism. Backus and his colleague Lon Echols led a congregation that met in a barn in Highland Park, Kentucky. Both were indicted by a US Grand Jury for espionage.

Frank Bartleman (1871–1936) was an outspoken evangelist and participant-reporter of the Azusa Street Revival. His immediate German ancestry and travels in Europe at the opening of WWI were combined with a theological and social critique of the various nations of Europe and the United States. While the *Pentecostal Evangel* carried his articles during WWI, at one point, under pressure from the US Government, readers were warned of his writings. He criticized patriotism as nation-worship and denounced the patriotic indoctrination of the young.

Arthur Sydney Booth-Clibborn (1855–1939) was a Quaker, turned Salvation Army leader and Holiness evangelist. Arthur was husband to Katherine Booth, son-in-law to founder William Booth of the Salvation Army. So profound was his influence on Pentecostals that the *Weekly Evangel* advertised his book by equating the pacifism of early Pentecostals to that of Quakers. His book arguing for Christian pacifism, *Blood Against Blood*, was banned in Britain during WWII. He criticized nominal churches that blessed swords, banners, and guns—instruments of indoctrination and killing.

---

1. These entries are heavily dependent upon *The New International Dictionary of Pentecostal and Charismatic Movements*.

About the Authors

Samuel Booth-Clibborn (1890–1969) was the son of Pentecostal pacifist minister Arthur Sydney Booth-Clibborn, who wrote *Blood Against Blood*. Samuel was an early Pentecostal preacher who claimed conscientious objection during WWI as a Quaker. He authored *Should a Christian Fight*. His book won praise among young Mennonites who read it during detention in Leavenworth. Surveillance from the FBI mistook Samuel for a Mennonite writer.

William Booth-Clibborn (1893–1971) was a British citizen living in the US during WWI and a conscientious objector to war. He was Quaker like his father, Arthur Sydney Booth-Clibborn, and Salvation Army like his mother, Katherine Booth, daughter of the founders of the Salvation Army, and his namesake grandfather, William Booth. He was a traveling evangelist and associated with the Pentecostal movement directly from at least 1920 to his death in 1971. As an evangelist he had apparent ecumenical qualities, speaking in Pentecostal and mainline denominations.

Stanley Frodsham (1882–1969) was an immigrant from England and editor of the *Pentecostal Evangel* at the time of WWI for nearly a generation.

Donald Gee (1891–1966) was a British Pentecostal who came of age and converted in the 1905 Welch revival and joined the Pentecostal movement as a young man. He was influenced by A. S. Booth-Clibborn and Frank Bartleman, and likely by Pastor A. E. Saxby, to lifelong championing of pacifism among Pentecostals. In WWI he was a conscientious objector, suffering as much derision for this as for other Pentecostal practices. He influenced Pentecostals around the world through teaching at colleges, writing extensively, and leading the Assemblies of God in England into the mid-1960s.

Frederick A. Graves (1856–1927) was a follower of John Alexander Dowie in Zion, Illinois. From there he became an early influential Pentecostal songwriter. He was father-in-law to Myer Perlman and his other children were influential Pentecostals. His use of religious music in the support of pacifism shows an early attempt to change culture.

C. H. Mason (1866–1961) was co-founder and long-time leader of the Church of God in Christ, the largest African-American Pentecostal church in North America. Mason was baptized in the Spirit at Azusa Street in 1906

About the Authors

under the leadership of William J. Seymour. He was closely monitored by the Federal Bureau of Investigation for his strong pacifist and interracial convictions. He was accused of preaching against WWI and jailed in Lexington, MS.

William Burt McCafferty (1889–1963) was an Assemblies of God pastor in Fort Worth, Texas, and an early principal of the Shield of Faith Bible Institute, which later became Southwestern Assemblies of God College. He argued for heavenly citizenship in contrast to nation citizenship, and believed fighting to be inconsistent with the doctrine of Christ.

Aimee Semple McPherson (1890–1944) was the founder of the Los Angeles-based Foursquare Church. She promoted gender equality, advocated disarmament, criticized the death penalty, and was an antiwar activist in the 1930s.

Charles Fox Parham (1873–1929) was one of the founders of North American Pentecostalism and champion of the Apostolic Faith. He is known for pioneering classical Pentecostal doctrine commonly known as speaking in tongues. Parham embraced Anglo-Israelism and eventually became racist in his views that culminated in his support of racial segregation. While Parham's teaching can be interpreted as racist, it was his disciple, William J. Seymour, who ultimately transformed the Pentecostal movement into an interracial and international movement. Parham also rejected nationalism, commercialism, war profiteering, and systemic violence.

Frederic B. Phillips (1869–1979) was a printer by trade and it was his own press that printed the first *Elim Evangel* in 1919. He was pastor of a small Pentecostal mission in Tamworth, Staffordshire. When Elim work transferred to London in 1923/1924, he moved with them and opened their new press, of which he became manager. He published the book *Is War Christian?* in 1937 and argued for Christian pacifism, believing Christians were to denounce war and all violence.[2]

H. Musgrave Reade was one of the founding members of the Labor Party in England before his conversion. He became part of the Keswick movement and later a Pentecostal pastor in the Apostolic Faith Church in England.

---

2. Beaman and Pipkin, 238.

About the Authors

William J. Seymour (1870–1922) was an African-American pastor from Louisiana and was one of the most influential leaders of early Pentecostalism. He was pastor of the Azusa Street Mission in Los Angeles where he supported interracial worship and gender equality. He was also the publisher of its *Apostolic Faith* magazine.

Ambrose Jessup Tomlinson (1865–1943) was General Overseer of the Church of God, Cleveland, Tennessee, and editor of the *Pentecostal Evangel*, where he promoted nonviolence. He had antislavery Quaker grandparents and he may have been a vegetarian. He criticized so-called "Christian nations," who during peace, looked down on bloodshed and murder, but, in war, saw human life as expendable. He lamented a time when bloodshed became honorable and killers and torturers (generals, politicians, soldiers) were honored with banquets, medals, and mansions.

Lillian Thistlethwaite (1873–1939) was the mother-in-law of Charles Fox Parham, a Quaker, before joining the Apostolic Faith, herself an evangelist. Parham named Thistlethwaite the first "general secretary of the Apostolic Faith Movement." She was the first woman to serve in an official leadership position within a Pentecostal organization.

1

"The Gold, White and Blue"[1]

Frederick A. Graves

1901

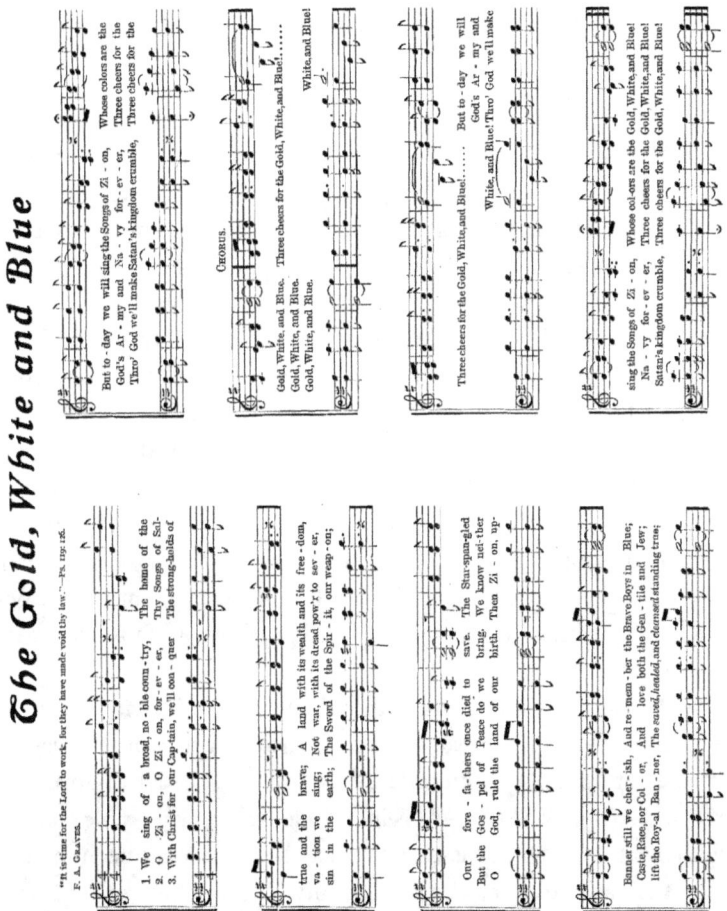

1. Graves, "The Gold, White and Blue." As demonstrated here, Frederick A. Graves, an early Pentecostal songwriter, used his music to support pacifism, racial, and social equality.

2

"Imminent Events in the United States"
Charles Fox Parham
1905

It would be unfair, indeed, to give the future history of other nations, and not give what prophecies there are concerning the United States. The wave of Bolshevism, now sweeping Europe, is as sure to reach this country in its devastating influence, as the plagues of Europe have always found their way to this country. You could no more quarantine against this power than you could against a pestilence originating in Europe. Besides, [the] United States, with her I.W.W.'s [Industrial Workers of the World] radical socialists and anarchist element, afford a more fertile soil for propagation of Bolshevism than Russia herself. The statescraft of the world offers no panacea for the cure of any remedial action to kill the germ that has caused Bolshevism. The gulf between capital and labor is so wide and deep that it can never be filled or salved [soothed] over by any government or capitalistic propaganda. Capital must exterminate and enslave the masses completely or be exterminated. The death struggle is on, and the working classes are determined to rule in the future, not only in Europe, but in the United States.

Two great forces are at war. An old civilization is dying. Her groans have been heard upon the battlefields of Europe. A new order arises from the masses of humanity, to utterly destroy the past order of government, church and society. The struggle is inevitable. The only possible conclusion would be victory for the masses. Our past civilization has been made possible by the early teachings of Christianity. The teaching of regeneration and holiness made possible lives of virtue. This, with the general distribution of wealth among the people has been the foundation for every past world's civilization. When these ceased, the civilization and the nations they gave birth to perished. Babylon, Egypt, and Rome fell when the wealth was gathered into the hands of the few, and gross immorality corrupted the people. To this, in Rome, was added the fact that most of the young men left the agricultural districts and crowded the cities. Ceasing to be food producers, they became only food consumers, their energies being expended upon building buildings and public roads. All these elements are driving our present nation to the same doom, coupled with the fact that today we not only have the wealth of the world gathered in the hands of the few, but piled up in combines and corporations and trusts, as recorded in the fifth chapter of James, as one of the proofs of the soon coming of the Lord. This quotation is taken from the translation of the New Testament into modern speech, "Come, you rich men, weep aloud and howl for your sorrows which will soon be upon you. Your treasures have rotted, and your piles of clothing are moth-eaten; your gold and silver have become covered with rust, and the rust on them will give evidence against you, and will eat your flesh like fire. You have hoarded up the wealth in these last days. I tell you that the pay of the laborers who have gathered in your crops—pay which you are keeping back—is calling out against you; and the outcries of those who have been your reapers have entered into the ears of the Lord of the armies of Heaven. Here on earth you have lived self-indulgent and profligate lives. You have stupified yourself with gross feeding; but a day of slaughter has come. You have condemned—you have murdered—the righteous man: he offers no resistance.

"Be patient, therefore, brethren, until the coming of the Lord. Notice how eagerly a farmer waits for a valuable crop. He is patient until it has received the early and latter rain. So you, also must be patient, keeping up your courage: for the coming of the Lord is close at hand. Do not cry out in condemnation one for another, brethren, lest you come under judgment. I tell you that the Judge is standing at the door."

The past order of civilization was upheld by the power of nationalism, which in turn was upheld by the spirit of patriotism, which divided the peoples of the world by geographical boundaries, over which each fought the other until they turned the world into shamble. The ruling power of this old order has always been the rich, who exploited the masses for profit or drove them en masse to war, to perpetuate their misrule. The principle teachers of patriotism maintaining nationalism were the churches, who have lost their spiritual power and have forsaken of God. Thus, on the side of the old order in the coming struggle, will be arrayed the governments, the rich, and the churches, and whatever forces they can drive or patriotically inspire to fight for them. On the other hand the new order that rises out of the sea of humanity knows no national boundaries, believing in the universal brotherhood of mankind and the establishment of the teachings of Jesus Christ as the foundation for all laws, whether political or social. For a long time the voices of the masses have vainly sought for relief, by agitation and the ballot, but the governments of the world were in the hands of the rich, the nobles, and the plutocrats, who forestalled all legislative action in the interest of the masses, until the wage-slavery of the world became unbearable; until the worm, long ground under the iron heel of oppression, begins to burn with vindictive fire, under the inspiration of a new patriotism in the interest of the freedom of the working class. Therefore, would it be considered strange if the over-zealous already begin to use the only means at hand for their liberty—by bombs and assassination to destroy the monsters of government and society that stand in the way of the realization of their hopes? It is impossible to inspire a Bolshevik or I.W.W. with patriotism or nationalism, for they belong to a new order whose basic principle is universal brotherhood. Thus, I say, we have come to the parting of the ways. On one side will be arrayed the government, the rich and the church. On the other side the masses. There is no possibility of harmonizing these two; one or the other will perish. Offering a better wage, or better home conditions, as a bribe to the working class is only an insult, for he is fighting for a principle, for universal liberty and the rule of the working class.

Over and over again, the Scriptures declare that when a nation forgets God, loses its spirituality, is lifted up in pride, oppresses the widow and the fatherless, and the hireling in his wages, and turns aside the stranger from his right, and fears not God that every such nation shall come to its end. When your cities are run with blood, God will destroy the nation. For the benefits in revenue, fines, license derived from saloons and brothels, this country has given scores of thousands of men to drunkards' graves, and hundreds of thousands of women and girls to nameless graves every year. No wonder Isaiah 66:16 says: "For by fire and by the sword will the Lord plead with all flesh: and the slain of the Lord shall be many."

Some readers may think this is a dark picture, yet how long can this nation go unpunished when the principal support of our city governments is blood money, drawn from the saloons and brothels, wine presses where the blood of your sons and daughters is ruthlessly trodden out. Thousands perishing year by year, with scarce a pitying eye, save of Him who shall render a judgment. Ere long Justice, with flaming sword, will step from behind the pleading form of Mercy, to punish a nation which has mingled the blood of thousands of human sacrifices upon the altar of her commercial and imperialistic expansion.[1]

---

1. Parham, *Everlasting Gospel*, 26–30. This piece was written on March 25, 1905.

3

Should a Christian Fight?

Samuel Booth-Clibborn

1910

Reasons Why A Christian Should Not Fight

A CHRISTIAN SHOULD NOT fight because through conversion or regeneration he has been born again into the kingdom of God and his citizenship is now in heaven. "For our citizenship is in heaven" (Phil 3:20). He must therefore obey first the law of heaven which is the law of love as opposed to that of revenge and slaughter; the latter often becoming the law of his country when at war. The Bible says: "Seek ye first the kingdom of God and His righteousness" (Matt 6:33), that is, we must put the claims of the kingdom of God far above those of our earthly governments and when the governments happen to contradict them, as in war, the claims of the heavenly kingdom should always have the preference.

What are the laws of the kingdom of heaven? What say the Scriptures? Throughout they are summed up in one word, "Love," it being the fulfillment of the law . . .

So love should be the law of heaven's representatives on earth, just as hate becomes the law of warring nations. Can the Christian consistently obey both? Impossible! He must either serve the God of love or the mammon of hate and murder. How can he pray for the salvation of a man while taking aim to shoot him down or while rushing madly on to plunge a reeking bayonet into his vitals? Impossible! Thus we see how impossible it is to try and reconcile the Christian's mission of love and salvation with that of modern warfare which is one of hatred and damnation.

[A Christian should not fight] because through the same blessed experience of regeneration the Christian has been baptized into "the Body of Christ" and now, as a member of that Body, he must love its other members irrespective of their nationality . . . If we are all brethren of the "household of faith," how can we hate and kill each other, which we are bound to do when fighting for our respective countries? What right have these countries to drag us into such a crime? Shall these doomed nations, who are compared in Daniel and Revelation to wild beasts, continue to tear asunder the Body of Christ? No! We, as Christians, must stand together and refuse to partake in their iniquity.[1]

[A Christian should not fight] because Christ sent His disciples into all the world, not to improve society by means of laws, nor to settle international quarrels by means of wars but only to save men . . . Just as the nations send their soldiers to the ends of the world to kill, so the Church has sent hers to save. Therefore, how can a missionary who has been laboring in a foreign land to save the heathen, suddenly turn around and kill the very same people because his earthly country happens to be at war with them? And yet, in spite of the incredible folly of such a course of action, some missionaries have actually in this present war become so blinded by the mammon of empire as to desert the army of salvation for that of destruction.[2]

[A Christian should not fight] because Christ instituted one supreme test whereby his genuine followers would always be known, "By this shall all men know that ye are my disciples if ye have love one to another" (John 13:35) . . . But just as love is the chief feature of the kingdom of heaven, so hate is that of warring nations. Now, can fervent love and bitter hate dwell together in God's child? Impossible![3]

War is often excused by pointing out that it develops such martial qualities as self-sacrifice, love of country, endurance, perseverance, etc., which qualities are often stifled by the ease, indolence and love of pleasure of peaceful times. There is no doubt a lot of truth in this, but what about the other side of the picture? What about the slaughter, the stinking bodies visited by worms, flies and vultures, what about the awful curses of the dying, the hideous hate for the enemy which the political leaders vigorously fan into a devouring flame; what about the spying and the lying and the censorship which is only Satan's modern trick by which the people are systematically deceived as to the true ghastliness of this dirty business? What

---

1. Booth-Clibborn, *Should A Christian Fight?*, 9, 14–15. Excerpts.
2. Ibid., 15–16.
3. Ibid., 16.

about the brutality, the vile lust which breaks loose, unrestrained in rape, the haughty price, etc., etc . . .[4]

Perhaps this may sound like sedition to some but it certainly is not, for it applies only to you as a Christian. We have no desire to undermine good and wholesome governmental authority or to show contempt and disrespect for the law of the land. On the contrary we deplore the increase of lawlessness everywhere and especially the lawlessness of this very war, and the reign of terror and anarchy which is bound to follow it. We firmly advocate a righteous and peaceful government as ordained of God (Rom 13), but we equally strongly denounce the wretched idolatry of nation-worship where parents sacrifice their young men on the bloody altars of the modern "Moloch" of Patriotism.

Our position, as Christians, is best illustrated by the noble prophet, Daniel. He was a perfect type of the Christian. He was a Jew of royal blood, but had to live in the mightiest heathen empire of those days. So we are the sons of God, yet have to live in the modern and mighty, though godless nations. Now Daniel became a mighty ruler in two successive kingdoms; in fact, head governor under two different kings. He obeyed the laws and respected the kings and proved the best governor these kingdoms ever had. Yet never once, in his career, did he stoop down for even a moment to worship these kings as gods, or their kingdoms as represented by their golden statues. He early determined that he would not defile himself and would worship only the true God of heaven. And he kept to this course although he was treated as a traitor and thrown into the lions' den for his stand.[5]

Some Objections Answered

Objection: But should we not obey the government of our country even when it forces us into military service and compels us to defend it? Did not Christ in Matthew 22:17–22 advise us to render tribute to Caesar and did not Paul in Romans 13:1–3 order us to be "subject unto higher powers"?

Answer: Yes, we should, when our government's laws are in conformity with those of God or when they do not hinder us in our obedience and service to Christ; but we should certainly not when they order us to disobey the law of Christ by butchering our fellow-men. The two passages

---

4. Ibid., 25.
5. Ibid., 39–40.

quoted in the objection will be seen to bear out this view when examined in connection with their context.

First as to Matthew 22:17-22. Beginning at verse fifteen, we find that the Pharisees had a council as to how they might trap Jesus and finally decide on the subject of the tribute money. Now the Jews were no more an independent but a conquered nation, a mere providence of Rome, and the people hoped that the promised Messiah would have overthrown Rome's haughty dominion. Jesus claimed to be that Messiah. If therefore, He advised them not to pay the tribute, which was a sign of subjection, they (the Pharisees) would report Him to headquarters as a revolutionist; but if He advised them to pay it, they would soon prove to the people that He was not the true Messiah; so they thought they had Him either way; but Jesus turned the tables and caught them both ways. As His rule over the Jews was not political but spiritual, they might as well continue to pay the tribute; yet, as His kingdom was of heaven, they should also render to God His dues. Jesus Himself gave men a wonderful example of this for He not only paid the tribute money to Caesar (see Matt 17:24-27, the incident of the fish money) but went further and literally surrendered His body to Caesar on the cross; for a Roman judge, Pilate, gave his consent, and Roman soldiers crucified Him. Then He finally surrendered His soul unto God and so should we do, for "as He was, so are we in this world."

Again, who is the greater, Caesar or God? If God be greater, He should have the first claim on our lives. His will should be first obeyed and such was the case with Christ. His meat and drink was to do His Father's will; Caesar's claim on Him was quite insignificant compared to His Father's. It should be so with us, His followers; we should see to it that we obey God first, and then earthly rulers.

The utter lack in Jesus of so-called "patriotism" is another striking phase of this narrative. There was Palestine—His own country, humanly speaking—reduced from a mighty independent nation to a servile province of Rome, and there was Christ, the lawful "King of the Jews" and the only One who was pre-eminently able to lead His people out of bondage into liberty, yet coolly advising them to continue in their wretched condition by paying the tribute. Had some of our military Christians lived in His day, they would perhaps have considered Him as very selfish, unsympathetic and unpatriotic; but, no, He had come to deliver them from a bondage far worse than mere political servitude. Should it not then be a matter of joy, instead of shame, that a few of His followers in these days are far more concerned over the salvation of precious immortal souls than over their earthly country's welfare? Therefore, to quote my father A. S. Booth-Clibborn's words in *Blood Against Blood*:

> The utmost that anyone can adduce from this passage in favor of war is that the body born within the bounds of an empire must, if needs be, be surrendered to the sovereign at his call. But that is precisely what the Christian does in allowing himself to be shot down by his king's orders, rather than to shoot. He is not a revolutionary, for he thus surrenders his body to Caesar and his spirit to God. He would surrender body and soul to Caesar in going to war.

Second, as to Romans 13 (entire chapter), Paul, after enjoining obedience to rulers, goes on to describe what types of rulers we should obey. In verse three, we read, "For rulers are not terror to good works," yet in Europe they have plunged nearly a dozen nations into a veritable hell. Verse eight says, "Owe no man anything but love;" but the Germans now say, "Owe no Englishman anything save hate." Again in verse ten, "Love worketh no ill to his neighbor, therefore love is the fulfilling of the law," but the rulers of Europe now say, "Hate kills our neighbor, therefore, hate is the fulfilling our law." Now are we, as God's people, to obey such laws formulated by such rulers? No! Most certainly not! Both must first conform to the scriptural standard before they can rightly claim our wholehearted obedience.

In the preceding chapter (chap. 12:17–21), Paul gives clear instructions to the Christians as to how he should treat his enemies. "Yes," object some, "his personal enemies but not necessarily his national enemies." Well, why did not Paul say so? He always took care to explain himself when necessary. (Is it not possible that the hidden reason for so many objections is a secret unwillingness to bear the consequences of Christian non-resistance?)

There is one more remarkable fact to be noticed, namely, the Apostles never taught one thing and lived another! Therefore, if they taught a slavish and cowardly subjection to rulers at all times, and under all circumstances, we have a right to look at their actions to see whether they really practiced what they preached.

Let us then turn to Acts 4:1: The disciples had just preached in the power of the Holy Spirit, so recently poured out on them. Thousands had already believed and the glad tidings were spreading like wildfire. Of course the priests, who were furious, "laid their hands on them" (v. 3) for they were the rulers. After hearing the Apostles' defense, they "commanded them not to speak at all in the name of Jesus." Did the Apostles obey them? No! For

Peter and John answered; "Whether it be right in the sight of God to hearken unto you more than unto God, judge ye, for we cannot but speak the things which we have seen and heard."

They put God first and therefore had to flatly disobey the government, so we may safely conclude that subjection at all times was not their teaching. True, theirs was not a refusal to enlist or fight, yet the principle involved was the same in both cases, for they wished to be at liberty to save men and we do not want to have that same privilege denied us by being made to shoot them down before we can ever save them.

This is not the only instance of holy lawlessness. The Apostles were always in hot water with the authorities for the truth's sake; so were the martyrs, so were the early Quakers, Mennonites, Methodists, Salvationists, and all other truly consecrated movements; and so will real, red-hot Christianity ever be, for its Founder predicted it. "If they have persecuted me, they will also persecute you" (John 15:20).[6]

Can a Christian Be Patriotic?

Before answering this question we must first inquire what is meant by "patriotism." The word "patriotism" comes from the Latin 'pater,' meaning 'father;' so patriotism is the love of and faith in, the Fatherland: that is, the purely natural love for the land established and defended at the cost of much blood by one's forefathers. This, then, is the primary meaning of the expression. There is a broader and secondary meaning with which we shall deal later. It is evidently quite human and natural to have a special affection for the country of one's birth, tongue, and upbringing.

A reason for the extraordinary hold "patriotism" has on people's minds and affections, as proved in wartime, is the careful and constant training of the youth of all lands in the history, heroism, beauty, nobility, and achievements of their respective countries. They are made to visit famous battlefields, and to admire monuments, shrines, and statues of national heroes. They are made to feel that "their country" is of course superior to other countries. They do not know exactly why, except because it is their country. History as taught through textbooks in use in the schools of the various nations, are also apt to suffer at the hands of their narrators; so that, strict impartiality being rare and difficult of attainment, the students are usually biased in the direction of glorification of the Fatherland.

6. Ibid., 54–59.

There is yet a deeper reason than training; for one cannot train what is not already there, in germ at least. Take for example the American people, and ask yourself the question, "Why is it, that after two years and a half of news, pictures, and even motion pictures of the war horrors, they are today rushing headlong into the conflict, so long deplored and condemned, with all the enthusiasm and martial ardor which but a short time ago seemed almost an anachronism?

The root reason is to be found in the universal longing of the human spirit for an exalted, noble, proud, ideal! What is that ideal? They do not know, because Satan "the god of this world hath blinded the minds of them which believe not, lest the light of the glorious Gospel of Christ, should shine unto them" (2 Cor 4:4). Yet they want something! Something worth living for and worth dying for! Something which shall raise them above the monotonous, selfish, sordid, grasping level of commercial competition, and the effort to benefit self, at whatever cost of ignoble strife or soul-defiling crookedness! Yes, something before which what is noblest in man, may, without loss, or self-accusing, or self-contempt, fall down and worship.

What is more natural than that this ideal should take the form of patriotism? Such an ideal has a completeness, which art, science, philosophy, and the like, can neither provide nor replace. In patriotism we find included, and raised to a higher power, the love of home, of wife, family and friends, and along with these the powerful motives ambition, progress, security, and an ever widening horizon.

Here is the secret origin of the defeat of the Pacifist and Socialist ideals. Their appeal seemed to be too much to the ease-loving , line-of-least-resistance, cowardly side of humanity; whilst the militarists, on the contrary, issued a summons to the field of valor, to the doing of heroic deeds, to the surrender of personal comfort, and individual advantage, nay of all the natural man holds dear, even to life itself!

In order to clearly understand the tactics of our wily adversary, it is necessary that we should remember that Satan is fully equipped with a working knowledge of the whole range of human sympathies, from the lowest to the highest; and that he knows well how to turn and twist the truest and loveliest instincts of the race into such channels that they may bring about its downfall. Just because "patriotism" appeals to the very noblest in man, Satan has his claws into it, and is using it as an agency of his kingdom; a stupendous engine for ruin and apostasy, by means of which the human race may be deceived and lured into the horrible crime of self–destruction.

Should a Christian Fight?

If man, the head and crown of all creation, be divided against himself, how shall his kingdom stand?

How many cowering shapes of worldliness, compromise, and carnality should we uncover, did we rend away the cloak of "patriotism" with which today the professing church of Christ is covering her unfaithfulness to Him who prayed that His followers might be One in Him, and that the world might know God had sent Him. In the name of "Patriotism" we are urged to go to war with other Christians. In the name of "Patriotism" we are to lie to other members of Christ; we are to rob our Christian brethren of other nations, we are to starve and bereave the little ones for whom He died! We are, in the name of "Patriotism," to kill, maim, and torture, (all in a spirit of love?), the children of our heavenly Father, for whom He laid down His life; leaving us a commandment that we should thus do in remembrance of Him.

As we have seen, God has given man a spirit as part of his nature. This spirit-nature was intended to commune with heaven just as the soul has intercourse with other human souls, and the body depends on the ground for existence. Ever since Eden Satan succeeded in turning our first parents from the worship of God to that of their own spirits ("Ye shall be as gods"), so His plan down the ages has been to substitute all manner of 'ideals' as objects of worship. In fact, his message to mankind is, "You may worship anything you like, as long as you do not glorify God!"

Well he knows that the outcome will be the coming worship of his own satanic majesty, as Antichrist. (Let me, in this connection, urge you to read the writings of Philip Mauro, on the present apostasy, the characteristics of the age, etc. I say it sincerely and independently, he is a true prophet of God. His books have opened the eyes of thousands to the deeper teachings of the Word. May they open yours.)

Under the spell of that evil influence, mankind has been worshipping the material world; "stocks and stones" (Jer 3:9), imitations of the human form, "graven images" and "molten images" (Isa 45:22; Deut 27:15); then great men, e.g. Darius whom Daniel was commanded to petition in God's stead (Dan 6:13); and now it is the fashion to worship "ideals."

Woe be it unto the man who is not in the fashion! When this godless world decrees a new fashion or belief or practice, all who want to "buy or sell" must bear this new "mark of the Beast" (Rev 13:16,17). "Be one of us," cries the world, "Go with the crowd!" Get on the band wagon, and show that you are a regular fellow!" Only, as the Apostle tells us, "that they may glory in your flesh." Everyone who does not bear, either in his house, person, or heart, the emblem of a blood-soaked, tear-splashed "Patriotism" is regarded as a traitor, a "slacker," or a weak-minded crank. "Being defamed, we entreat: we are made as the filth of the world, and are the offscouring of all things unto this day" (1 Cor 4:13).

Shall we now pass in review the chief reasons why a Christian cannot be "patriotic" (according to the world's standard of patriotism)?

1. Because the aims of present-day "Patriotism" and true Christianity are diametrically opposed. The one cause of this war is the pitiful delusion of a Golden Age without God. The Kaiser thought he could attain this end by the method of forcibly-feeding the nations with German "Kultur!" In this he has [manifestly] failed. The Allies want to reach the same goal by "Making the world safe for democracy." They too will ignominiously fail, because they are not practicing what they preach. Whilst talking very loud about "fighting for the freedom of Europe" they are crushing religious liberty at home. In England conscientious objectors have been shamefully treated, and in this country we, too, are heading for the abolition of free speech, free assemblage, and free press. On the other hand true Christianity (not the apostate churches) is preparing for a millennial reign of her King and Lord—our adorable Lord Jesus—by separating herself from the "Kingdoms of this world" until He takes possession of them (Rev 11:15).

2. Because present-day "patriotism," whilst appealing to the highest in man, is really very earthly! A few glances on the pages of history should easily convince the most obstinate. Oh, the rivers of blood which have flowed for possession of a few square miles of territory here and there! And to what purpose I pray you? Has righteousness increased in consequence? As my dear father says: "They are all fighting for what does not belong to them. The Fatherland is really *Father's land*; 'the earth is the Lord's and the fullness thereof' (1 Cor 10:26)."

3. Because nowhere are we told in the New Testament to be "patriotic." On the contrary, it clearly teaches us, "The little flock," to have nothing to do with the ideals, aims and methods of "this present evil world" (Gal 1:4) of which this "Patriotism" is but a branch. The result of this attitude, namely, in that the world hates us, is also shown. Said Christ: "If the world hate you, ye know that it hated Me before it hated you. If ye were of the world, the world would love his own: but I have chosen

you out of the world, therefore the world hateth you" (John 15:18, 19). Paul declared: "But God forbid that I should glory, save in the cross of our Lord Jesus Christ, by whom the world is crucified unto me, and I unto the world!" (Gal 6:14). James affirmed: "Ye adulterers and adulteresses, know ye not that the friendship of the world is enmity with God? Whosoever therefore will be a friend of the world is the enemy of God" (James 4:4). John the Blessed said: "Love not the world, neither the things that are in the world. If any man love the world, the love of the Father is not in him" (1 John 2:15). " . . . and this is that spirit of Antichrist, whereof ye have heard that it should come; and even now already is it in the world" (1 John 4:3). In Revelation he also wrote: " . . . and all the world wondered after the Beast" (Rev 13:3). Some say Paul was "patriotic" because he once or twice said he was a Roman. Well, if he was, it must have been a queer kind of "patriotism" seeing that Rome imprisoned and beheaded him.

4. Because "Patriotism" as practiced nowadays in the world is nothing less than Rank Idolatry. The papers are full of articles describing how to wear, salute, kiss, bare-the-head, and stand up to flags and emblems. The early Quakers felt so strongly on this point of giving unto men or things the reverence and worship which belonged to God alone, that they would not take off their hats to anybody, not even to Kings and Judges. Let the "children of disobedience" worship flags, and monuments, and heroes, dead or alive—they are doing the best they know, poor things! God knows I am not sneering at them. Their courage and self-abnegation is enough to make us luke-warm ease-loving Christians blush for shame—not that we don't join their cause but that we are so slow in fighting *for our own!* Their enthusiasm is all the more pathetic as it is futile. But *you* cannot join them—*you* have been "bought with a price" (1 Cor 8:23). Therefore follow the Thessalonians of old in that they "turned to God from idols to serve the Living and True God" (1 Thess 1:9). Listen to God's Word as it thunders: "Thou shalt not make unto thyself any graven image, or any likeness of anything that is in heaven above, or that is in earth beneath, or that is in the water under the earth: thou shalt not bow down thyself to them, nor serve them (Exod 20:4–5). This verse of the Ten Commandments condemns the worship of the flags, emblems and crests of the nations in very lucid language. For instance, the Japanese and American flags reproduce the rising sun and the stars of the firmament or things "in

heaven above." Also the crests of England, Germany, Russia, China, etc., have lions, eagles, dragons, etc., or "things in the earth beneath."[7]

7. Ibid., 73–80.

4

"Victory"

Lillian Thistlethwaite

1912

> "Be not overcome of evil, but overcome evil with good."
> Rom 12:21.

THE MAJORITY OF THE human race from the beginning of time to the present age, though vaguely acknowledging a Supreme Being, have practiced the law of the "survival of the fittest;" "might has been right" in personal conflict and national achievements, and the power of "brain or brawn" the mark of superiority under the general competitive systems.

At intervals during the world's history, men of humble minds, chosen of God and quickened by His spirit, have dared to stem the tide and reveal the greater law of non-resistance, picturing to at least some degree the character and attributes of God and his requirements for humanity.

But when the fullness of time was come, God sent forth his Son, made of a woman, made under the law, "to redeem them that were under the law that we might receive the adoption of sons." In the Son was manifested the "fullness of the God-head bodily." "God was in Christ, reconciling the world unto himself," yet, as was prophesied of Him, He came to be rejected, crucified and slain, that His purposes might be fulfilled [through] perfect "obedience even unto death," hence the victory over the law of sin and death [through] non-resistance, and the living faith which gave him power to lay down his life and power to take it again.

To the Captain of our salvation alone belongs this overcoming power, and in him we are made more than conquerors, as in obedience to Divine Law, we "resist not evil," "love our enemies," "bless and curse not," and by His spirit are we enabled to say, "Father forgive them, they know not what they do." Thus by taking up of the cross and walking under the new law of love, which is service to humanity, the self is slain, as the "ego" has lost his life for Christ's sake and the gospel's and found the "more abundant life," and the welcome of the Maker: "Inasmuch as ye have done it unto the least of one of these my brethren, ye have done it unto me," ushers us into the "joy of the Lord" as "many sons are brought unto glory."[1]

---

1. Thistlethwaite, "Victory," 1–3.

5

"War! War! War!"
Charles Fox Parham
1914

TO MURDER A FELLOW-CREATURE! To receive therefore even less than thirty pieces of silver, and perhaps live to receive the plaudits and honor of a more cowardly country and imbecile nation; for that nation is imbecile which retains its existence through the struggling exploits of war. We hang our heads in shame to see Christian nations and individuals yield themselves to the embrace of the Moloch-God, Patriotism, whose principal doctrine was honor (?), there to have consumed in that death struggle the feeling of philanthropy and humanity; spending millions to build the fires for the consummation of these virtues, while the cause of Christ languishes, heaven loses, hell opens her jaws, and so-called Christian nations feed (by war) to satisfy her gluttonous appetite.

How much more far reaching the influence would be, for time and eternity, if nations and individuals could really become imbued with the teachings of Jesus, whom they profess to follow, and spend millions and the men in the world's evangelization. Yet while thousands of men will volunteer and suffer hardships and privations of an earthly war for glory, few, indeed, will volunteer and endure the slightest privations for the Master's kingdom and eternal glory. Where is your faith, brethren? Will we hide ourselves in the rocks and mountains in earth? Will we hide ourselves in the rocks and mountains in shame, when He appears, or shall we arouse ourselves and prove our loyalty by our works, lift up a standard for the people, carry aloft the blood-stained banner of King Emanuel, and enlist, then, when the war is over, have to stand aside, or with the victorious redeemed army, though tattered and torn, march in triumph in the grand review of the King of Kings?[1]

1. Parham, "War! War! War!," n.p.

6

Blood Against Blood
Arthur Sydney Booth-Clibborn
1914

You find the cover [of my book] gruesome? It is designedly so, in order to be absolutely true to fact. The final expression of the two alternative and extreme remedies for sin at the opposite poles of spiritual forces—life-giving and death-giving—the Blood shed once and for all, the endless blood-shedding,—are gruesome. The Cain principle and the Abel principle, the Beast life and Lamb life, War and Calvary, the massacring hosts, and the holy army of martyrs—each utters, at its own culmination, a truth which has been written in red on black all down human history, and which cannot be written on white in grey or in green, whatever the new theologies or theosophies, the new peace systems, or the new social reformations of modern days may say or do.

The descending stream of blood represents that coming from the pierced side of the Saviour on the cross. The transversal stream bursts from a bayonet wound made in the breast of a Christian by a fellow-Christian. They form a cross signifying that Christ is crucified afresh by these so-called Christian wars. They are at right angles to indicate that they represent systems of force, salvation and safety which are mutually excluding and never reconcilable.

On the back is the spear of Caesar which made Christians, and the Christian gun and bayonet which make infidels. The first opened in the Saviour's side "the foundation for sin and uncleanness." The second opens for converted Christians a new fountain of hellish war in which they can get back all their sin and uncleanness, with a large addition.

Were a system required to ensure the spiritual blinding and backsliding of simple-minded Christian's, and to march them back into deeper sin than that which they had left, none could have been devised more perfectly adapted to the end in view, than that of war, the military system, and official association which the empires of earth and their cruel quarrels.

The Anglo-Boer struggle presented one of the most terrible features of war, in circumstances unparalleled for centuries. Family ties, homes, and homesteads were put into the mill of militarism, and ground up as never before in the name of sacred Christian obligations to God and country. Among the Boers the destruction of Mauser-wielding [i.e. arms-carrying] fathers and mothers, brothers, and sisters, and the dying of little children in Concentration Camps had to go on under each other's very eyes, while among the English the death of loved ones went on at an immense distance. Each opposite extreme of the destruction of home ties was thus reached. And as if to crown the climax, it all occurred in the presence of the heathen, while above the Christian armies engaged in mutual destruction, and as if to give them its blessing, waved the standards of the Christian churches, in two hostile halves.

Christianity is the only remedy to war. Not a bloodless gospel on the one hand, not an adulterated evangelicalism on the other. It must be Blood against blood.

All intermediary systems, all efforts to mix these two forces and bloods by either Christian reformers and reformed pagans, have only one effect in the long run, to create martyrs for the truth by adding to the great life of all time, and thus perpetuating the persecuting spirit in new forms, and the wars of men under new "religious" cloaks.

The remedy for war, and the sin which produces it, must be as extreme, as costly and as painful, as the disease it has to remove. It is the fashion just now to consider the bloodiness of Calvary as too unpleasant a subject for polite ears. Our modern humanitarianism would do away altogether with the doctrine of the cross. The vulgar spitting, the crown of thorns, the mocking enthronement, the seven hours hanging on wounds, the pierced side, are disagreeable subjects. For if they mean anything they mean "the exceeding sinfulness of sin," and the completely "lost" state of the most comfortable moralists around us, apart from personal salvation by the cross of Christ . . . Do we really realise what our evangelical Christianity teaches? It is extremely "extreme." The truth must be rejected or defended—not with supineness, but with the utmost energy—for Christless theologies, or reformed religions, which have reformed Christ Himself, are knocking loudly at the door. There is a charge contained in the book of the London City Temple pastor which has lately appeared that will have to be met. We cannot pass it by. It blocks up the narrow way completely; and it is well that it does so. Evangelical religion ought not to try and pass beyond. It is the fifteen centuries of awful "Christian" wars for which he holds orthodox Christianity responsible. It has never dared to say war was wrong. On the contrary it has blessed the swords, the banners and the guns!

Christian father! Hold up your hands; open them; then get your baby girl to hold up one fat group of five fingers; then get your eldest boy to hold up one finger; put the fingers all in a row, and count them: there are sixteen. They represent the centuries since "Christians" first began to become soldiers, as a, to them, normal profession. Your boy's forefinger can represent the present century. Will it one day point on a war map the path by which a position is to be stormed at some awful sacrifice of life, with a Christian "courage" renewed by Japanese example—or will it press a button by which a German Dreadnought and its thousands of heroes will "go to glory?"

Our evangelical doctrine is too extreme to be easily altered. It levels down genteel and vulgar sins into one black mass. It declares that the most honoured of earth's unregenerate moralists or scientists, the most generous of its millionaire supporters of social work—have equal need of salvation, by the most awful means possible—the bloody cross of Christ, yes, equal need with the most degraded criminals of our slums, wallowing in the back-wash of our selfish civilisation.

And at the opposite pole? Will it not now at least declare the equivalent truth, or else haul down once and for ever the red flag of Calvary? Will it not dare to affirm that the gruesomeness of Christian war has nothing Christian in it? That is arose solely and exclusively with the great apostasy? That the martyr and not he who kills is authentically Christian? That it was only as Calvary became gradually meaningless in practical life that the other red commenced to blot the fair annals of Christian history, hitherto unstained, even though martyr blood underlined every phase of witnessing upon its pages? Will they not recognise that the progress of apostasy is clearly defined in history, and has been universally recognised by evangelicals? Let us read into it the language of modern flags and rags—gorgeous war and squalid slums.

At the close of the first century we see patches of discolouration upon it. Our Lord Himself describes some of them in His messages to the seven churches. The process went on, ever larger portions of the flag turned from red to pink, from pink to a dirty white. At last only in corners and along the haft did the glaring red linger. Then came the Roman Emperor Constantine. There had been gradations naturally between, but let us accept him as the typical figure in the great change then about to take place. Paganism and Christianity became fused—or to change the simile, the lamb lay down beside the wolf. The result was inevitable. The process just described became inverted. Gradually "the banner of the cross" began to become red once again, but with a dye of another origin. "Christian war" with the sword began to be looked upon as normal and necessary. The world "must be won." Had not Christ sad "Go ye into all the world and preach the gospel to every creature?" Was not the sword a good instrument wherewith to clear the way for the cross? The other way had been found too narrow, the other gate too straight. "You can't live at that level," people had said. "Such extreme ideas are not practical." And so the progress went on, until at last it issued in the Crusades and their corollary, the Inquisition. The washed-out flag of Calvary had been re-dyed. This time it was with the blood of Cain, not of Christ. And meanwhile in holes and corners, in caves and dens of the earth, a reopened New Testament was preparing once again the true flag of Calvary, dyed with the blood of the Master, and of those endeavouring with faithful, though faltering footsteps, to follow their crucified King! It was being raised aloft by Albigenses, Waldenses, and Hussite Moravians.

And now, we are once again at an hour of crisis. Peace, peace is the cry on all hands. Away with the Christianity which makes these divisions they cry. We are all one! These good moralists, these Piccadilly *roués*, are all on the natural upward road. All are equally engaged in a quest after God—unregenerate "millionaires" of money, or of political power, or of human will force—are all one, and can share equally in the social effort of man to save his own world on material lines. Calvary's red flag is meaningless and therefore valueless. So speak the new socialistic forces and theologies.

Can this be all right to us common-place evangelicals? No! To us above all others an inexpressibly awful delusion must lie behind such views. But how are we to make a stand against them? Get back the glaring gruesome complete red of Calvary's flag. That is all. Separation! "Come out and be ye separate."

Get back to true "Christian war" by getting away from the false.

Look at so-called "Christian war." What can be more deluding?

The inexpressibly awful realities of the distant battlefield are hidden from the eyes of the English, French, and German homes behind the gorgeous uniforms, the splendid music, the proud martial air of carnal superiority borne by masses moving with mathematical precision, accompanied by mighty mowing machines of death, provided by the highest Christian science of destruction. They pass by under gorgeous flags double crosses upon them. On, on they move to the great harbours where float in their somber glory the awful Dreadnoughts, and on and on across God's health-giving briny seas, on to the grim, gruesome climax. And meanwhile the officer occupies a superior position in the ball-room, and the highest national honour is heaped upon the returning conqueror. A place is kept for his tomb in St. Paul's or in Westminster Abbey.

They have had recourse to worldly arms under a Christian cloak. The highest honours of the world are theirs. Meanwhile the lowly, lonely evangelists may wield his (absurd) sword of the Spirit, the Word of God (forsooth!) in the corners of the city or the world, and preach a Saviour whom the highest culture of the day crucified between two thieves!

Earthly empires have always sought to insure their own lives and perpetuation in power at all costs. They are actuated by purely animal or beast instincts. They can know nothing of Calvary. The sword is their natural emblem, for it embodies their policy of insurance. They must crucify the Christ principle, whose central force is a life insurance of an exactly opposite kind.

And what would happen if, in a London Queen's Hall, a Paris Trocadero or an Unter den Linden some extreme preacher of salvation by Blood were to stride across the downward course of our modern Christianity, and say that Christian war with worldly weapons was a ghastly crime against Christ? And if he were to add, as I venture to point out in this book, that the price for which Christ was sold was exactly the price of a modern "Christian" gun, and if to give emphasis to his holy protest, and to show that he was not going in his own name, but was treading upon holy ground, he were to take off his shoes from off his feet. What would happen? You know. He would be called mad of course.

And if he were to go on to say that such an unnatural alliance of opposite principles, carried into the political sphere and expressed by that between Christian England and Pagan Japan for the "peace" of the East was utterly anti-Christian, and a sign of a culmination in our country's apostasy, what would be his lot? You know. He would be called bad of course. He would be "a traitor."

And some would perhaps go to endeavor to get his friends or even his wife or children to say he was both mad and bad and thus doubly secure his moral death warrant.

Such action would be probably out of time and out of place. We are no longer in an outward dispensation such as the Jewish when symbolic action was a suitable form of preaching and was understood by all. But we have only to imagine the case to obtain a true picture of the reception such witnessing would meet with.

History, carnal and spiritual, always does repeat itself.

There thus comes hours when "charity," "breadth of view," "Christian submission," "love of peace," are terms which can easily hide culpable supineness and disloyalty to Christ and the red flag of Calvary.

But oh! shall we not arise as never before in the holy revolt of true love, church of the Crucified and only Redeemer? Shall we not—reversing the old salutation of the Roman soldiers as they passed before Caesar, on their way to war or gladiatorial struggles, *Ave Cesar! Morituri te salutant!* "Hail Caesar! they who are going to die salute thee"; shall we not passing before the cross cry the same to our King—even at this hour crucified afresh in all the great capitals of earth and their empires? This is no mere figure of speech. Whoever is faithful in this age to all that Calvary means will surely meet with Calvary treatment. The form of crucifixion may differ; but the spirit will be the same. But shall we not be willing thus to help "in our own bodies on the tree"—on some modern pillory of disdain—to compare the holy cycle of revelation? Earthly empires dream the red flag of revolution. Let none of us dread the red flag of Redemption. Under it alone is safety.[1]

---

1. Booth-Clibborn, *Blood Against Blood*, 44–52. Excerpt. The *Weekly Evangel* frequently encouraged pacifism by advertising Booth-Clibborn's antiwar publication. For an example, see "Blood Against Blood," 3.

7

"The Character of the Church"

William J. Seymour

1915

A CHURCH CONSTITUTES A kind of spiritual kingdom in the world, but not of the world; whose king is Christ; whose law is His word; whose institutions are His ordinances; whose duty is His service; whose reward is His blessing.

In all matters of faith and conscience, as well as in all matters of internal order and government, a church is "under law to Christ" (1 Cor 9:21); but as men and citizens, its members must "submit themselves to governors" (1 Pet 2:14), like other men, so far as shall not interfere with, or contravene, the claims of the divine law and authority upon them. They must "render unto Caesar the things that are Caesar's, and unto God the things that are God's," remembering that God's claims are supreme, and annihilate all claims that contradict or oppose them (Matt 22:21).[1]

---

1. Seymour, *The Doctrines and Discipline of Azusa Street*, 93.

8

"Should Christians Go To War?"
William Burt McCafferty
1915

THERE APPEARED IN THE columns of the *Christian Evangel* (no. 70) an article headed "Is European War Justifiable?" in which the question was asked "should a Christian go to war?" and then the argument is set forth justifying Christians in taking up arms on behalf of their country, if the country happens to be in the right as far as the cause of the war is concerned. But it seems to be forgotten that Christians asked this same question once before.

In Luke 22:49, the disciples asked Jesus, "Lord, shall we smite with the sword?" They prayed, but, instead of waiting for an answer, one immediately drew the sword and went to battle cutting off the ear of one of their opposers.

We will meet the argument that it is only natural that we defend the weak against the "bully" as was brought out in the illustration used by our English brethren, which appeared in the columns of our little paper. The illustration goes further to say "that in case a great wild hooligan came in and began to maltreat the family, that it would be right to fight, praying to God at the same time," or words to that effect. Now, that is what the disciples did, prayed (Luke 22:49), but, instead of waiting for an answer, they began with carnal weapons to defeat the bully (the opposing force which came against Jesus).

Now brethren, we ask the question "Shall we fight with the sword?" or "Shall a Christian go to war?" let us wait for an answer from God. Let us not begin to reason from the natural point of view, but wait for a "Thus saith the Lord."

What was the answer of Christ to the disciples (Christians) to this question? (Matt 26:51) "Put up again thy sword into his place." This is what God is saying to the Christians of today, "Ye followers of the Prince of

Peace, disarm yourselves" for "the weapons of our warfare are not carnal" (the musket, sword, [sledge] gun or cannon; 2 Cor 10:4). And we are not contending with flesh and blood. Our warfare is waged against the host of spiritual darkness. Our armor is not the spiked helmet, the suit of mail [armor], etc., but the helmet of salvation, the shield of faith, the breastplate of righteousness. Our feet are not "swift to shed blood" but are shed with the preparation of the Gospel of peace (1 Thess 5:8, Eph 6:11, 17). Oh Christian, "put up thy sword, into his place, for all they that take the sword shall perish with the sword" (Matt 26:52).

Jesus, to teach the disciples that the warfare of the Christian was not with carnal weapons, gave them an object lesson, saying, "When I sent you without purse and scrip and shoes, lacked ye anything?" They said nothing. Then said He unto them, But now he that hath a purse let him take it, likewise his script (go, give alms, relieve the suffering, etc.; Isa 58:8–11; Jas 1:27; 1 John 3:17, 18) "and he that hath no sword let him sell his garment and buy one" (Heb 4:12), and they, with ears tuned only to the natural said, "Lord, here are two swords," and Jesus, to teach the lesson that was recorded for the Christian world, said, "It is enough" (Luke 22:35–38) and now the time has come, "Lord, shall we smite with the sword?" Thou art weak shall we defend thee against the strong? Thou art in the right, shall we defend thee against the wrong? "Shall we smite with the sword?"

The argument that we must go to war on behalf of the weaker nation because of its being in the right, is not consistent with the doctrines of Christ. It is also against the teaching of Christ to fight in self-defense. "For even hereunto were we called, because Christ also suffered leaving us an example that we should follow His steps, who did no sin (violence, Isa 63:9) who, when he was reviled, reviled not again, when he suffered, threatened not, but committed himself to Him that judgeth righteously.

Paul gives a better way of peace than by gaining it through bloodshed. "I exact therefore, that, first of all, prayers, intercession, and giving of thanks be made for all men; for kings and for all that are in authority that we may live a quiet and peaceable life, etc." The Christian is not of this world even as Christ is not of this world. John 17:16. Our citizenship is not of this world, our citizenship is in heaven. Phil 3:20. We belong to the Kingdom of God and the Kingdom of God and the kingdoms of this world are not allied. When two kingdoms go to war with other nations or kingdoms, their interests are mutual, they are allied one with the other. Christians are separate from the world and are subjects of God's kingdom, a kingdom of peace which shall be established upon the earth when the Prince of Peace returns.

We hear the Spirit say, "If any man have ears to hear, let him hear. He that leadeth into captivity shall go into captivity. He that killeth with the sword must be killed with the sword." Here is the patience and faith of the saints. Shall we fight with the sword? Shall we as Christians go to war?[1]

---

1. McCafferty, "Should Christians Go To War?," 1.

9

"The Present Situation"
Ambrose Jessup Tomlinson
1915

IT IS ALMOST USELESS to say that the world is in one great turmoil. All who keep posted on the events of the day are apprised of this fact without repeating it here, but we call attention to this as a kind of introduction to what may follow.

Great nations are in war against each other. As nations they are doing the very thing that they forbid by their civil laws. Bloodshed and murder were forbidden by their laws and punishable by death or imprisonment, and the perpetrator was looked upon as a mean low down character, but now these same nations are engaged in a wholesale slaughter accounting human life as of no value, and the bloodshed has become an honor. If this is not [villainous] then we are without expression.

Boys and men snatched away from their homes and loved ones are rushed off to war and shot down by thousands like cattle and hogs in the slaughter pens. Homes are broken up never to be repaired; property destroyed by the ravages of war and people who were toiling pleasantly along a few weeks ago are reduced to poverty and starvation today.

Women are helpless, little innocent children are nothing more than vagabonds on the earth. Yesterday the nations of the earth were boasting of their high state of civilization, holding their peace conferences and planning to step right into a state of millennial peacefulness; today they are plunged beneath the surface of a crimson sea and bathing themselves in the blood of uncivilized barbarism. So called Christian nations have lost their identity as such and fallen into their own snares.

They are proving that their profession of Christianity was only a sham and the vilest grade of hypocrisy. They had just as well sail under their own banner (that of the antichrist) and never again disgrace the worthy name of our Lord and Savior Jesus Christ by trying to hide under His name.

This is a time for Satan. Millions of souls are driven by the cruel war lash into the slaughter-pens of hell. This, however, is probably no worse in God's sight than the hypocritical absurdity of much so-called Christianity that prevails in both North and South America as well as the other countries of the world. It is probably no worse after all than for the multitudes to be rocked to sleep by the pulpit masters that sing their lullaby's over their congregations every Sunday morning, and lead them to the vaudeville in the afternoon and tell them they can't live without sin, which is to say, they can serve the devil all the week. Then when they come to their dying hour and their sun is setting they are persuaded to believe they are going to be carried by the angles into the sweet haven of everlasting bliss.

Taking everything into consideration the present situation is a puzzle to the minds of eminent men. Many are finding satisfaction in studying prophecy and applying it to the present situation, but as they are so far apart in their ideas and applications it proves that they are making misapplications and that they are without divine wisdom and inspiration after all.

People have become so wise in their own conceit that they do not know that God has hidden these things from the wise and prudent, and they are only groping around in darkness while they are boasting of their findings. Many people who are now making a great display as Bible scholars would show more godly wisdom to sit down with their hands over their mouths and act like fools till they get a real revelation from God and a head and heart full of godly wisdom and understanding. "Let no man deceive himself. If any man among you seemeth to be wise in this world, let him become a fool, that he may be wise" (1 Cor 3:18). "Consider what I say; and the Lord give thee understanding in all things" (2 Tim 2:7). "Trust in the Lord with all thine heart; and lean not to thine own understanding" (Prov 3:5). "Be not wise in thine own eyes: fear the Lord and depart from evil" (Prov 3:7).

It is dangerous to accept a man's teaching who himself has not departed from evil and placed himself in an attitude toward God that He can instruct and inspire him and reveal to him the things that are hidden from the natural man. Paul declares that "the natural man receiveth not the things of the Spirit of God: for they are foolishness unto him: neither can he know them, because they are spiritually discerned" (1 Cor 2:4). When God hides a thing from a man he can't find it, no matter how much he may search, unless he meets the conditions that are required. It would be better in the end for many of these wiseacres [a know-it-all] to leave their watchtowers of self-importance and take a quiet walk down the slopes of humiliation and meet the Lord Jesus and obtain from Him a good cause of salvation and receive the Holy Ghost, then they could be fit for service in leading others to Christ.

While the multitudes of "up-to-date" people are studying the war problems and engaged in the political strife incident more or less to all nations and have their minds wrought up to a high pitch and inflated with patriotic (?) zeal from reading the newspaper reports, is a good time for us to humble ourselves a little lower and go among the common people and work for the salvation of their souls. We believe it a timely thing to say that more time should be given to saving the lost. Let us buckle on the armor a little tighter and go into the soul-saving business with more zeal, courage and determination than ever before. We need to work with such furiousness to pull men's souls out of the fire that people will look on us with amazement and wonder what strategy we are going to use next.

Now is our time to strike the fatal blow to false religion and hypocritical Christianity, by simply preaching the plain gospel and testifying to its effect upon the human heart and life. Don't strive, don't argue or dispute, don't vilify, but with a shipload of love for souls, tell them if they sin they are sinners, and if they do not repent they will perish. Be firm and gentle at the same time. Cry aloud, and spare not. Give sin no quarters where ever it may be found. Hate sin with a perfect hatred, but love the sinner and pull him out of the fire hating the very garments that are spotted by the flesh.[1]

---

1. Tomlinson, "The Present Situation," 1. Excerpt.

10

"The European War"

Frank Bartleman

1915

SOMEONE HAS FACETIOUSLY ASKED, "Why pray for peace? The Lord did not start this mess." Very true. And yet innocent people can pray for peace. No, God is not responsible for this awful war. But sin is. It is the unrestrained outworking of the sin principle in man. Possibly less people will be ready to deny that the human race is fallen after this carnage. It is certainly hypocritical and blasphemous to pray for peace if we are in any sense responsible for the continuation of the war. This nation has it largely in her power to stop the fighting. At present we have many millions of dollars' worth of orders for ammunitions and arms alone from nations at war in Europe. We are keeping the whole thing going. The nation, the voters, the church members, could stop this if they would insist upon it. Hence we are a nation of hypocrites when we claim to be neutral. Our neutrality does not deliver us from our greed for the dollar. We are willing to receive these millions of blood money. We had better pluck out the stars from our flag and instate dollar marks in their place.

But, "Be sure your sins will find you out." This is as true of nations as of individuals.

They say corporations have no souls. But the individuals comprising them have, and God punishes them. And so with nations. Nations receive physical punishment, as nations, for nations, in themselves, as such, have no future. It is certainly inconsistent for the nations at war to pray for peace while they keep on fighting. All are equally guilty in this. They started the trouble. How can God stop it until they themselves quit fighting? The fact is each one hopes to whip the other before he quits the conflict. This cannot be, naturally. They cannot all win. Some think the Pope himself started this

"The European War"

war, to acquire the dictatorship in the end, in spite of all his prayers and [pretenses] at wanting peace. God knows.

If Germany beats Russia, this may result in the freeing of the Poles, the Finns, and the Jews, and of the Russian people themselves from the awful yoke of religious intolerance and despotism in the end. God grant it. We have prayed long for this. Sinners are set to punish sinners. And this sin works out its reward. Russia's intolerance calls for vengeance upon her. But it may have been necessary for England and France to attack Germany for her punishment also, as a counter balance. Germany has greatly sinned. And she might become a menace to the whole of Europe when she bad whipped Russia were she not herself thus reduced by France and England, who themselves in turn are also punished. They act upon one another for general judgment.

The emblems of the nations are wild beasts and birds of prey. How fitting! When Nebuchadnezzar fell, through pride, God took away the heart of a man and gave him the heart of a beast. The fallen nations have the heart of a beast. They have fallen through pride. They are being humbled and reduced today. Their motives are altogether selfish in this struggle. Some good will be wrought out of it for some innocent people, in the midst of the awful evil. But the misery will be something awful in its total for multitudes of others. The innocent suffer with the guilty. This seems unavoidable in large measure in this fallen condition. In the aggregate may we not hope that God will ultimately get glory. The nations must be punished.

The Balkan Slav nations are afraid of Russia. They prefer to see her defeated. Their sympathies and hopes lie toward western civilization. Russian tyranny is semi-barbarism. But they dare not oppose her. Hence their waiting attitude in this crisis. Russia is doing all she can, with the Allies, to force them. They prefer Germany to Russia. Italy has been simply diplomatic. She is slick as oil. She wanted to be sure to be on the winning side. The Allies finally offered the greatest inducements. She sold out to them and broke her word with Germany. Each one is after spoils. There is no honor or principle in the matter. Japan has got her share and is content for the present. The Balkan states want their share in the end. All have the heart of a beast.

There is no love between Russia and England. In fact they are deadly foes. But they are friends for the present for mutual gain. How shallow and hypocritical are all their pretensions at honor and principle. They gull the simple people with such nonsense. The fact is the chance of war was very welcome with them. In England, Russia, France and Germany Socialists were greatly threatening the government. In France the Socialists were about to disband militarism. And in England they were facing a crisis with Ireland on the Home Rule question. War was a welcome issue to all. It was their only hope of uniting, through patriotism, their badly severed forces. And the poor people must spill their blood to save the rulers fortunes.

England, the leading Christian nation is found in the very worst of company. She is in contract with infidel France, atheistic Belgium, heathen Japan, despotic Russia, and murderous Serbia. Not at all good company. If we are known by the company we keep, and if birds of a feather flock together, the outlook is not at all good for England. She is willing to drag the whole world, heathen and Christian, into the war. She has Belgium of the Congo atrocities. France of the murder of the innocents. Italy, the seat of the "Beast," the Pope, and Russia the persecutor of God's ancient people the Jews, with her intolerant Greek Church system, all with her. How can she have God with her? On the other hand Germany is yoked up with the Moslem world, the "False Prophet," the greatest enemy of the Cross, the Crescent. Oh, what a spectacle to a suffering, dying world! Hell has broken lose truly. England herself must fight Russia ultimately.

No nation is so responsible as England, though they are all filling up the cup of their iniquity. England has been honored of God above all. She has been unfaithful to her trust in India. She has catered to the heathen systems of religious worship there. Then at home God has a controversy with her. The servant class must be emancipated. The lords must turn their great "preaerves" into potato patches to feed the starving thousands of the common people. God is done with class system in England.

We speak without fear or favor. England has been jealous of her young German rival.

We favor no country. The militarism of Germany must be broken. But it cannot be broken successfully by navalism, or a greater militia. That would be changing horses only. The Prince of Peace must crush it. England took advantage of Germany to jump on her when both her hands were full. She had waited for the opportunity. It was trade rivalry. She has crushed Spain, Holland, and France before her. England controls all the great ocean highways. Gibraltar, Port Sald, Aden, and Singapore. She will control Panama if she can, with Japan to help her.

Germany no doubt is ambitious to rule Europe. It would be better with her than with Russia. But better with neither as absolute ruler. Hence England and France have been allowed of God to set upon Germany. All must be weakened. They are getting too strong. God is denied and defied. Each fights for selfish motives, if France had broken Belgium neutrality in attacking Germany, England would never have gone into the war for that reason. No one believes that excuse.

Patriotism has been fanned into a flame. The religious passion has been invoked, and the national gods called upon for defence in each case. What blasphemy! Men who before lived in peace and satisfaction now hate one another unto murder. It is simply wholesale murder. It is nothing short of hell. And yet they glorify it. The awful after-results cannot yet be realized. Each nation is afraid to let go or show signs of a desire for peace lest it be misunderstood for weakness and advantage be taken of it by another. And thus they struggle on, each fighting for his own life, believingly. They have staked all upon the outcome. It is war to the death. Hate is fanned into fury. Each fights for first position and supremacy, that they may not need to repeat the struggle. They hope to win for all time.

Truly all beautiful theories about the rapid development of the human race through their own efforts are not fallen. They are using all progress and development in science, etc., to blow men into hell, and yet there still live some fools insane enough to tell us that all this carnage is working for the further development of the race in the end. As far as the race is concerned it is a crazy contradiction, needing no further contradiction.

The sexes will be unbalanced. Awful sin will follow. We will have nations of murderers after this war. A generation with their hands stained with the blood of other human beings. They will be used to scenes of blood and violence. Who can compute the effect of all this in the hardening of the people? Whole nations will be tired with hatred in heart and mind against one another for coming generations. Not only men but the women and the children. This is the awful toll of war. There will be little left of this generation but physical incapables to perpetuate the nation. The taxes will be awful. And if they begin again to prepare for future revenge and reparation how can they stand the strain? It is all madness. Man cannot save himself. The Prince of Peace must do it.

There is no possible excuse for the murder of these people. Hundreds of thousands of innocent ones are being slain on the battlefields of Europe today. Men are murdering one another with absolutely nothing to gain. They are losing all. They have no possible reason for hating and killing one another. Why should they create widows and orphans for one another?

What crime have all these innocent ones committed? None whatever. They are simply blinded. Blinded by sin, blinded by ignorance, blinded and controlled by their leaders.[1]

---

1. Bartleman, "The European War," 3.

11

"Present Day Conditions"
Frank Bartleman
1915

Nine years ago the Holy Spirit began to lead us into the Book of Acts and show us the meaning of that Word that had been hidden since the backsliding of the church in the early centuries, as to its fullness. We have now had approximately, as concerns the world situation, "seven years" of plenty, under the "latter rain" outpouring. Have we laid up "corn as the sand of the sea" for the time of future famine that has already burst upon us? Or have we wasted it in riotous living, selfishly spending it upon our own spiritual indulgence, not using the presence and power of God to build ourselves up and become established for the trying times so soon to come. If the Pentecostal people had made the right use of their "corn," there would not be so many going into error today. The "seven years of famine" have already set in. A "famine for the Word of God."

Today the Holy Spirit is leading us into the Books of Daniel and Revelation, unfolding their meaning. The time for their opening has come. They are being fulfilled.

Judgment Has Begun

"The wicked shall be turned into hell, with all the nations that forget God." The nations are being judged. Belgium for her Congo atrocities, France for her infidelity and devil worship, Germany for her materialism and militarism, England for her hypocrisy, bullyism over weaker nations, and her overwhelming pride. Belgium is an atheistic nation, practically without marriage rites or religion. France is even more guilty than Sodom and Gomorrah. She is more responsible. Germany has almost ruled religion out of her churches, and the admission of God out of her schools. The German babies are brought up on beer in the bottle. The English children are kept alive on whiskey mixed with strong tea. Extreme poverty forbids sufficient food for poor children even in peace times. The inequality between the rich and the poor is simply awful. And so the world groans under the oppression of sin. It groans to be delivered. The earth is heaving in war throes to get rid of its tyrant and oppressor man.

Moral Degeneration

After the Balkan war Bulgaria considered seriously the establishing of polygamy. She was short of men. The women greatly outnumbered them. Her men had gone to feed the cannon. She needed more cannon fodder. And so it will be throughout Europe after this present war. The proper relation of the sexes is being upset altogether. And this means chaos and further crime. Awful sin will follow. "Thy men shall fall by the sword. Seven women shall take hold of one man in that day" (Isa 3:2; 4:1). We are facing that day. The nations are today bidding for "war babies." They are to be declared legitimate. God's law and right to interfere in the matter of promiscuous and unrestrained co-habitation between the sexes is to be denied altogether. They must have more cannon fodder. A dark day had broken in on this poor old world. Carnegie's dream of universal peace is about ended. It was only a dream. The complete demoralization of the nations has set in. There is no longer national honor. No self-respect, or respect for others.

American Lords

The United States has a score of kings where European countries have but one. That is about the only difference. We are ruled by money gods. Our next year's wheat crop is sold and the price we must pay for bread [is] determined before even the seed is planted in the ground. Thus our wheat gamblers control us. We are helpless in their grasp. They gamble with the lives of the whole nation. What will God do with such a nation as this? They claim, and gamble with the future. If this is not tempting God, then there is no possibility of doing so. We are slated for damnation as a nation.

"Present Day Conditions"

Warning Judgments

But, "the hour of her judgment is come." "Go to ye rich men, weep and howl" (Jas 5). A gigantic plot was nipped in the bud only a few weeks ago in New York City in which it was planned to blow up with dynamite Vanderbilt, Rockefeller, and Carnegie.

God is humbling the price of man again. The "Great Northern" on her first, proud trip through the Panama Canal took a record run to Hawaii for dessert. Her passenger list was made up of millionaires and the "upper crust." She returned hastily without completing the excursion on land, a funeral ship. Two of her proud party were killed on their way up the mountain side to visit the Volcano.

God warned Italy some time ago with a terrible earthquake calamity, just as she was about to go into the war. The soldiers and supplies intended for the campaign were required for the urgent need of succoring her own suffering people. A noted Italian premier, while lecturing eloquently for the war at Milan at the climax of his exhortation while the people were vociferously applauding him, suddenly lunged forward and dropped dead. Again God has spoken in warning. And yet they have not heeded. They are also bent on receiving their share of the general judgment. They refuse God's offer of mercy and warning.

Recently the proud Lusitania (a parallel case with the Titanic) has also sunk beneath the waves. A torpedo bored its way into the bowels of the great vessel loaded with ammunition and arms for the destruction of the Germans. In less than half an hour the boat was gone. The ammunition exploded. It turned into an American torpedo. The ammunition came from America. And yet we complain because Americans were killed on the vessel. Oh, consistency, thou art indeed a rare jewel! America's besetting sin is her money and greed. "Be sure her sin will find her out." It will sink her in the end also. It always does. Judgment time has come. "God is not mocked." We are making [strenuous] efforts today to prepare for war also. And yet our hands are tied. Why is it? God has tied them. We are being reserved for our share of the judgment. We are fattening for the slaughter. God is holding us helpless. We have taught the European nations how to war. We have invented and manufactured almost all the hellish instruments used in modern warfare for the destruction of men. And we are keeping the nations of Europe supplied both with ammunition and provisions for the warfare carried on today. Yet we ourselves are admittedly absolutely unprotected and helpless to defend our own selves against a foe. What does it mean? It spells judgment for us.

Vain Petitions

The churches are praying for peace. But there is no answer from God. Even the warning time seems about ended. Terrible times are just before us. Men cry 'peace, peace,' but there is no peace. It is time for judgment. Rome is raising up her head again. If ever the Moslem, the "False Prophet," declares a 'holy war' it will be now. It is his last stand. Even England, titled "Defender of the Faith," has at last sold out to Rome. Old King Saul is forsaken of God. He is backslidden and turned to the "witch of Endor," the heathen, nations for instruction and support.

Missionary effort is well nigh paralyzed. And small wonder. What have we to say to the heathen in the face of the present example of the recognized Christian nations? Are they not calling the heathen to help kill each other? Humanity and morals are simply paralyzed. Hate and murder fill the world. What shall we say to the Indian, the Turk, and the Japanese? Oh, the delusion of war. "War is hell!"

End Nearing

But soon it will be said to the inhabitants of this world, "he that is filthy, let him be filthy still" (Rev 22:11). Character is crystallizing. Final judgment of the nations has begun. "They knew not until the flood came and took them all away." And so it ends with the awful and increasing indifference of today. Even the message of warning seems almost ended. They are "slumbering and sleeping." The end is near.[1]

---

1. Bartleman, "Present Day Conditions," 3.

12

"Christian Preparedness"

Frank Bartleman

N.D.

"Seeing that these things are thus all to be dissolved, what manner of persons ought ye to be in all holy living and godliness, looking for and earnestly desiring the coming of the day of God" (2 Pet 3:11, 12).

This is Christian preparedness. Calamities are happening every day that before the war began would any single one of them have shaken the world. They fail to disturb us today. We are getting accustomed to them. As a nation we are now also preparing for war. Is this Christian preparedness or the preparation of which God speaks?

The most hypothetical and blasphemous spectacle the world has ever been called to look upon is that of the so-called leading Christian nations calling each upon God to damn the other today. And the worst influenced in all departments is that of preachers crying out for preparedness for war and for revenge from multitudes of our most popular and influential pulpits throughout the land.

Scholars tell us that up to the fourth century soldiers were denied the Sacraments of the Church, because they were professional shedders of blood. Today the Church is crying for blood. In Westminster Abbey the Generals who have led their soldiers to the greatest slaughter are canonized as the highest rank of saints today. And this is true in all state churches in all lands.

There is no greater inconsistency extant than for the Church of Jesus Christ to go to war. Her business is to preach, not murder. The weapons of our warfare are not carnal. No, not even for self-protection. Did Jesus Christ protect Himself? Or did He teach us to do so? We have got to trample all the laws of Jesus Christ under foot before the Church can go to war.

War is not God's way for the Church. Ours is different, opposite calling in this dispensation. But we have neglected our calling. That is why the Church goes to war. We have not preached the Gospel. We have not converted our enemies. We have not gone to them with salvation. They now come to us, to destroy us. It is our judgment. We have not believed God. We have not obeyed Him, tarried for the enduement, and gone forth to witness. Our time has come to reap the punishment for our neglect and disobedience. It is no good seizing the sword now. The world is coming back at the Church at the end of the days, the "last days."

The opportunity is gone. We have neglected it, and we must suffer the penalty for our failure. In saving others we save ourselves. This we have neglected and failed to do. The end is upon us now. There is no remedy for our failure. We must be offered up. We must be martyred. Or if we seize the sword we must perish by the sword. That is God's word. I am speaking of the Church now. Our martyrdom after this sort will not be as honorable as those who have suffered at the stake in former days. They bore a faithful testimony. They sealed their testimony with their blood. We are to suffer largely for our disobedience. Or perish trying to defend ourselves, denying the faith altogether.

Think of the millions of professing Christians today murdering one another for a little bit of territory, or denying the other even the right to live. A right that God has given equally to all men. And they blindly call on God to help them. Is there not room on God's earth for all nations? The Gospel teaches us to live and let live. War is an indictment of God. God has provided plenty. The greed of men alone is responsible for its unequal distribution. The crime of the ruling classes is overwhelming. It cries to heaven. And vanity stalks abroad. There is little here for the true child of God. Think of Charlie Chaplin, the popular Movie Actor, getting around half a million dollars and over, for one year's salary, while millions are starving.

How can the Church be patriotic for this world? Has God made men to love or to destroy one another? What example are we supposed to set to the heathen? What influence is there left to hold violence in check when the Church goes to war? Or in what sense do we differ from the world, or the brute creation, who destroy one another? And what saving virtue is there left in the Gospel when this point is yielded? There is no argument on earth or in heaven to justify the Church in the attitude of war.

"Christian Preparedness"

Every preacher preaching war is condemned from his own mouth. And likewise every Christian. Nor can they preach "national preparedness." They can only preach the Gospel. Some preachers would not be quite so popular if they preached the Gospel. However, they would be more "beloved" in heaven. How much Gospel have we taken to Mexico? How much money have we spent to carry the Gospel to the Spanish speaking people?

We have simply gone in there to get more gold, to carry the riches of Mexico out with us. Honest, that is what we have been after. And that is what we are after today. The church has piled up riches. And her riches will destroy her. They should have been spent preaching the Gospel in Mexico, and other countries. They have been withheld from God, and now we are going to lose them. We lose everything that we withhold from God, and now we are going to lose them. It is His property. He requires it of us. We shall lose much of it now in guns and ammunition, probably, to kill Mexicans. We shall lose much of it in war taxes. Human governments are after gold, not after saving men's souls. We are not going into Mexico to save the people, but to kill them. Is that God's call? Is there no strength in God? It has always been the policy of the stronger nations to spoil the weaker ones.

Who knows how close Japan stands behind Mexico today? To strike Mexico may mean that we shall be smitten by Japan. God may have ordered it for our chastisement as a nation. We have withheld the Gospel from Mexico and Japan. We may get judgment before we get Mexico or her gold.

We have been sending food to Belgium. The Church has been appealed to and donated largely in this act of mercy. But we still ship great cargoes of guns and ammunitions to continue the unparalleled slaughter, need and suffering. What has the Church to say to this? Has she condemned it? If not, why not? What does God think of this? It is inconsistency, abominable hypocrisy.

When we deal death to others, furnish ammunition for the wholesale slaughter of millions in Europe, why should we squeal if a few ammunition factories get blown up in our own land, or such cargoes on the way? Is it a Christian game? No, it is all for gold. We are in the game of war. And American lives are no better than European. We must swallow our medicine. We want the dollar. Fire will burn, and murder brings murder. It is a law of God. It is presumption to pray for protection along this line. Chickens come home to roost. And so will much of our ammunition, with interest.

When leading nations engage in wholesale murder among themselves there is no moral law to check red handed revolution in the country. All are in the game. One is lawlessness, robbery, and murder among nations, the other that of individuals. There is no difference whatever.[1]

---

1. Bartleman, "Christian Preparedness," 114–15.

13

"Is Christian Civilization Breaking Down?"

Frank Bartleman

1915

COUNT OKUMA, THE HONORED and venerable Prime Minister of Japan, made the statement at the outbreak of the European war that "we are witnessing the end of the civilization of Europe." The world has associated the national life of Europe so closely with Christianity that it has been customary to refer to the European nations—especially some of those that are now in war—as examples of what "Christian civilization" can do for a nation. These countries, together with America, have been held up as models to China, Japan, and the people of other non-Christian lands as examples for them to follow. Their great universities have been pointed to as models; their laws giving liberty to the masses and assuring justice to all have been taken as an illustration of what Christianity does for a nation. It is not surprising, therefore, that now when these great so-called "Christian countries" are locked in a bitter struggle with each other in what is proving to be the most widespread and general war this world has ever seen, that the question is asked—Is Christian civilization failing? Is Christianity a religion that is of any advantage to a nation?

The last of August a sermon was preached in the Turkish mosque of Saint Sophia in Constantinople, in which the Mohammedan audience that filled that great mosque, once a Christian church, said: "I bring you good news. There is general war raging all over Europe. We have long prayed, saying, "O Lord, let these infidels quarrel with each other," [and now] God has listened to our prayer. Beyond twenty millions infidels are killing each other with most devilish instruments. May God make it more." And all the people said, "Amen." The Mohammedan uses the word "infidel" for Christians.

An editorial printed in a Chinese paper in Peking, late in August, among other significant things, said:

"They point to the West and bid us gaze in wild surmise on the kingdoms and principalities of Europe, the pomp and [pageantry] of its varied life, its cities, wealth, industry, and commerce, its magical inventions and discoveries, its science, and the vast generalizations of a people resolved to wrest all her secrets from nature and thus—presumptuous thought—to conquer God. But even so, what do all these things profit if the harvest is war and slaughter of strong men and broken hearts of women and pain and suffering?"

It is no wonder that the heathen rage and the Mohammedans imagine vain things when they witness what seems to them to be the foundation of Christian civilization failing and the entire structure crumbling.

Christianity has not broken down, but men have failed to be Christian. The civilization of the so-called "Christian countries" has been essentially pagan in all of the relations of nation to nation and country to country, and it is in these relations that international war is carried on.

Some years ago, in the heart of Kurdistan, I administered the communion in a building that could seat one hundred and fifty people. The communicants numbered something like sixty or seventy. Along the wall of the church were ranged guns of various sizes, and knives, with quite a scattering of two-edged swords, and every communicant has strapped close by his side, during the entire service, a two-edged dirk [dagger]. These had come to the house of God that day in groups, thoroughly armed, and, after the service, they trooped out, forming themselves into triple, quadruple, or sextuple alliances, or whatever the case might be, in order for their self-protection. In that country every individual, whenever he traveled, armed himself, expecting that the first person he met upon the road might be an enemy with whom it might be necessary for him to wage a deadly warfare for his own protection. That was pagan civilization as related to the individual. It was a civilization where the individual had to look out for himself, since there was no protecting government to assure him of justice.

In many places in India and China, villages and elites have walls, and in the earlier days the people of one village or city went out in attack upon another village or city, striving to gain supremacy. Therefore [the] city was armed against city, village against village. In Japan, before the adoption of the constitutional government, the various clans which made up the Japanese nation were armed one against another, and often fought. All these were but outward forms of pagan civilization.

Europe has built up its national life on precisely the same basis, and, for the same reason that the Kurd armed himself before starting for Church, or the Indian or Chinese city built at great cost a wall for defensive and offense purposes, each nation has prepared itself to fight with a sister nation, with expectation that sometime it might be necessary to wage war. And so great armaments have been built up, navies have been constructed, soldiers have been trained and prepared to fight. This condition has prevailed among all the nations of Europe, and, as the armament was increased, suspicion increased, fears were multiplied, and the suspicion and fear led to the enlargement of the armies and the development of their equipment. For the carrying out of these plans the best intelligence of Europe has been requisitioned to prepare the most mighty engines of destruction possible and to manipulate them with the highest scientific and mechanical skill.

Who would dare say that this is Christian Civilization? Where between the covers of the Word of God, in all the teachings of our Lord Jesus Christ and all of his apostles, is there one word of warrant for attaching the name "Christian" to such a society and to such a state? On the other hand, our Lord Jesus Christ taught the blessedness of the peacemaker, that violence should not be resisted with violence that those who take the sword shall perish with the sword. That is Christianity, and only a civilization built upon the basis of the teaching of Jesus Christ can bear the name "Christian." Europe is plunged in war today because its civilization was unchristian, because it was preeminently and glaringly pagan. Europe is bathed in blood because it has violated the natural and Christian law of the social world, and it is reaping only the results of its contempt of the law of God by which he insists nations as well as individuals shall be governed.[1]

---

1. Bartleman, "Is Christian Civilization Breaking Down?," 3.

14

"Pentecostal Saints Opposed to War"

The Weekly Evangel

1915

THE PENTECOSTAL PEOPLE, AS a whole, are uncompromisingly opposed to war, having much the same spirit as the early Quakers, who would rather be shot themselves than that they should shed the blood of their fellowmen. Because we have given this bit of war news is no reason that we are in favor of war, but rather that our readers may bare some knowledge of how the war is actually affecting our own people, who, through force of circumstances are compelled to be in the midst of the terrible conflict. Indeed, some have already urged us to arrange for a great peace council among the Pentecostal saints to put ourselves on record as being opposed to war at home or abroad. We are told that many German brethren, when commanded to take up arms, have refused to do so and have suffered martyrdom as a consequence. Others, because they have been compelled to do so, have gone with the armies, not knowing how to do otherwise, but praying that God will save them from taking the life of any man. The Gospel Publishing House is now in possession of a powerful book entitled "Blood against Blood," written by Arthur Booth-Clibborn, an English Pentecostal brother who has been the means of a glorious ministry in Germany before the opening of the war. This book we are offering to our readers for 55 cts. postpaid, and we recommend that you purchase it and become imbued with the spirit of its contents, in a complete opposition and protest against war and the shedding of blood.[1]

---

1. "Pentecostal Saints Opposed to War," 1. This is an anonymous article likely written by either E. N. Bell (Editor-in-Chief) or J. R. Flower (Office Editor).

15

"What Will the Harvest Be?"

Frank Bartleman

1915

DOUBTLESS NO HUMAN BEING yet knows the final outcome of the present world war, now raging. For one year the awful carnage and destruction has continued and yet the end does not really seem to be in view. The scene is ever changing. It is like a kaleidoscopic view of its constant variations. There seems to be no great gain on any side. The exact final result no one can yet prophesy. One thing is certain, awful loss and suffering is the sure outcome. Already the devastation to human life and property is overwhelming. The world is staggered as its unparalleled proportions in destruction. The human mind is incapable of grasping the real magnitude of this [season] of desolation. The harvest is bound to be one mass of crippled, crushed humanity. And the souls that have been damned will be awful.

What is the gain? Apparently nothing in the aggregate. Who can replace the men and material destroyed in this war? It is all destruction. Is not the world large enough for the whole human race to live off. If not, God must have made a criminal mistake. The present war carried on by the nations, professedly in the name of God, is an indictment of God by them. They charge God with a failure to provide sustenance for them. But what are they doing? Not only destroying men but their sustenance also. It is a hypocritical, hellish lie from them.

Not a Holy War

This war is not a holy war. It is the result of pride, greed, jealously, hatred, hypocrisy, etc. The men or set of kings, leaders, war lords, capitalists, politicians, diplomats, manufacturers, bankers, etc., who are responsible for the present war, with its awful suffering for men, women and children, its effect on humanity in the hindering of the Gospel, the sending of men to hell, etc., will have as hot a place in the regions of the damned as old Nero or any of the demons will ever have. The crime of the ages is now being perpetuated upon us.

The whole thing is a game of chess, with the nations as the players. Kings and leaders, capitalists, are the chess men. They play their nations as the stake. Rulers for their private purse, bankers and financiers of the world for gain, munition manufacturers and provision merchants, all work together in this game. Flesh and blood of the common people, soldiers, are either forced or hired to do the fighting. The souls of men are the material used up in the scrabble (Rev 18:13).

It is true the enormous mass of Russian prisoners of war now in Germany will return home after the struggle is ended with new ideas regarding liberty of conscience, etc., gathered from a better form of civilization, and with a better knowledge of and respect for their neighbor. But the heathen religions of the world, held by the brown, yellow and black races, are going to be harder to influence and overcome after the present example of failure by the white nations. Nominal Christianity has certainly proven a failure. State religions have proven the curse of their peoples. It is in the name of these national gods that they have been inspired to go to war. It really seems as though the horses of Rev 6, war, famine, pestilence and death, were already going forth, so great is the magnitude and horror of this conflict.

The Menace of Rome

If Italy were to win, "Victor Immanuel" would have it in his power to restore the Pope to secular authority again. And he would be more likely to do so than to honor Christ between the two. But he is not sure to win. In spite of the pretensions of his name, he may lose. God is not giving His kingdom to earthly rulers at any rate. They are all fallen, kings and kingdoms. England believes assuredly that the present Prince of Wales, one of whose name is David, is the ruler whom God has chosen in Holy Writ to sit on the Throne of David. This is her conceit. But she sent an ambassador at the beginning of the war to represent her at the court of the Pope in Rome, a thing she had refused to do for five hundred years previous. It is before the Pope and not Christ that she is kneeling also. God is not going to give the Throne of David to her.

There is no righteous nation in the earth today. England, whose religious pretensions are the greatest today, has stolen most of her possessions from the weaker nations. She is the greatest of sea pirates. It would be amusing, if not so criminal, to hear her prate of the righteousness of her cause against Germany. God's day of judgment will bring a fatal indictment against all the present nations. Only ignorant people are impressed with such twaddle. England has stolen the navies of the seas. She has stolen the seven seas themselves. Like the dog in the manger she proposes to keep them. America will find that out someday to her sorrow. We would not for a moment think of crediting Germany with having altogether pure motives, but if she is able to force England's grip to the dividing of the freedom of the seas among the nations she will have accomplished at least one benefit for humanity. The object of all earthly nations is purely selfish.

England stole the diamond mines of South Africa from the Dutch Government. She has not recently met a worthy foe. Blucher won the day for her at Waterloo, against Napoleon. Wellington was never more pleased in his life to see a friend than he was to see Germany coming to his help at that time. Today England is fighting with the French against her. Friends today, foes tomorrow. Oh, the fickle friendship of earthly nations! Belgium is England's natural protection against Germany. She is the buffer between, that keeps Germany from the Channel. But England's sun is surely setting. God has decreed it.

Honor to Whom Honor is Due

The sins of Germany are many. But she has accumulated what she has largely by hard labor. She is in a wonderful state of organism and cultivation. Such a nation cannot be destroyed. England must follow her example. Instead of preserves for the supporting of the rich, for hunting, cricket, etc., she must plant potato patches. Poverty stalks abroad over all in England. Her populace is in a most precarious condition for the bare necessities of life for the most part. It will require all her resources after the war to save her.

In Germany cities even the vacant lots are all planted with vegetable gardens. Every foot of ground is utilized and developed to the utmost. They have built their nation with the sword in one hand and trowel in the other. A ring of steel has been forged around them by their neighbor nations. Germany has known since the uniting of her providences that she must someday fight for her life against her jealous neighbors. Hence her constant preparation for defensive warfare. Her armament has been made to keep pace with her development of industry as a nation. By carrying her defensive at time into the country of her foes, and on strategic grounds, she has saved her own life, industries, and [peoples]. When the facts are finally known it will be revealed that she did not strike the first blow in this world war. In self-defense she was driven to it. God will be judge and witness. The trust must be told.

Little Justice or Mercy

It is not worthwhile for Christians to wax warm in patriotism over this world's situation. There is little justice or mercy in the fallen nations. England cut the cable at the beginning of the war that connected Germany with the world. She then started with the press in a campaign of lies. First impressions regarding facts were altogether misleading. A tremendous sentiment was thus early created by England against Germany. World sympathy was with England. Will God stand for such unfairness? Our American press has been controlled largely by English capital. In fact there has been little difference between our press and that of London. We have for the most part been a mere echo of London, Paris, and St. Petersburg. The public has been given what the leaders chose and directed. And Germany has had very little chance to tell her side of the story. Even her reports have had to pass through English hands and censor before they reach publication. She has been isolated from the world by England. Her populace is to be starved out. It is a crime to have been even born a German. The voice of explanation or appeal has even been denied her. Early Roman law was more just than that to the accused ones. Will God condone this?

Before the reports in our press can be believed we must first search out the motive. And that is impossible to do. Men are paid to write to bias the public. There is no effort for justice. In fact the whole game is played for selfish conquest. American capitalists, leader and manufacturers are as deep in the mud as the others are in the mire. Politicians rule the day. And politics is rotten. We are a nation of grafters. People who do not know this are people who have never taken the trouble to consider the situation. But God will judge us.

The German press is known to be peculiarly solid and trustworthy by her people. This I know to be true having lived in the country. There is the greatest contrast between the press and spirit of Germany and that of

England. Again honor to whom honor is due. Facts must be spoken. They will meet us at the judgment. In Germany the people are solid, sincere, and desperately in earnest. Of course they are in the wrong sometimes also, and they are likely to stand by their country, right or wrong. England will do that also. America will do the same thing. There is not principle enough in any of these countries to overcome that.

In England, in the beginning of the war, the press and spirit of the people was most boastful and superficial. It was pride and arrogancy, mixed with unreality and theoretical professionalism. When I reached New York and read the morning papers I thought I was back in London. That explains itself. We had sold out to England.

Danger to America

This strange infatuation that has laid hold of us against facts and justice will prove our ruin. England is determined to have the Panama Canal. Her diplomats are much more shrewd than our own. We are almost at war with Mexico. From the beginning England has sought to undermine our influence in Mexico. A powder train is laid for us. Japan is ready, with England, to help Mexico. She wants the [Philippines] and Hawaii. And yet we seem blind to it. Our greed thoroughly blinds us. "Be sure our sins will find us out" before God. Our war party, powder and ammunition manufacturers, etc., see their opportunity as this crisis with us. A fortune in war supplies and provisions awaits our merchants, manufacturers and capitalists. They are willing to plunge our nation even into war to get this. Our rulers dare not say no to them if they hope to retain their offices. Who but God can help us?

Call to Repentance

Hence we need a call at this time as a nation to repentance. I suppose it will be always possible for our nation to hire men to slay others. But the spirit of patriotism is not going to burn very bright in a people who are ruled by grafters. The game is not worth the candle. Especially when it is for mere love for some other nation. A foreign invasion would be a different thing altogether. What prosperity we are experiencing as a nation today is being derived from furnishing shot and shell to the Allies across the water to kill Germans. I suppose that is a righteous business with God if we are to accept the testimony of our leaders and newspapers. We have killed off about all of our American Indians.[1] What we have not killed outright we have starved through some big grafter at Washington diverting the appropriations of the Government for their support to his own pocket. And we have fed our soldiers in our recent campaign against Spain with rotten canned goods to enrich the same big grafters. The appropriations for provisions for our own soldiers has gone the same way. Who can be expected to respect such an unprincipled situation. Will not God deal in judgment with such a nation as this? Most assuredly! We have stolen the land from the North American Indians, and the bread from our own national support, our own soldiers. What worse can we do? Are we a righteous nation, deserving the protection of God? Let me answer. Our wrong to the black people was avenged in blood. What will the next be?

We are living on blood money today and trying to wash our hands in innocency in the matter. But it will not come off. Sin has blinded our nation. Yet we hope to escape the consequences. It is madness. Whom God would destroy He first renders foolish. Our sins have brought us to an unholy position where to back down threatens war with the Allies, and to go forward war with Germany. God is not with us. With Canada on the north, Mexico below, Japan on the west, and England east of us, there is no seeming escape but by fleeing to God, through the narrow gate to a true repentance, July 30, 1915.[2]

---

1. Bartleman's attempt to be against racism was not widespread at this time. Moreover, his critique against US "democracy" was considered very seditious at this time.

2. Bartleman, "What will the Harvest Be?," 1–2.

16

"Our Heavenly Citizenship"
Stanley Frodsham
1915

IN A RECENT ISSUE of the Evangel it was emphasized that the children of God should preserve an attitude of strict neutrality to the warring nations in Europe. But it seems to the writer that the Word of God teaches something deeper than that. We frequently sing, "This world, this world is not my home, this world is not my resting place." This is true. The salvation of Jesus is a deliverance from "this present evil world." (Gal 1:4.) It is a translation into the Kingdom of God's dear Son (Col 1:13). The Cross of Jesus Christ is the place where the saint and the world separate forever (Gal 6:14).

When any foreigner comes to the United States and seeks to be a citizen, he has to renounce his loyalty to his former king, so when one comes into that higher kingdom and becomes a citizen of that "holy nation" (1 Pet 2:9.), the things that pertain to earth should forever lose their hold, even that natural love for the nation where one happened to be born, and loyalty to the new King should swallow up all other loyalties. Our attitude to all the nations of this earth should be that of Ruth and Moab when she told Naomi, "Where thou goest, I will go: and where thou lodgest I will lodge: thy people shall be my people, and thy God my God." The new birth makes one become a true Jew, for the Word of God declares that he is not a Jew which is one outwardly, but he is a Jew which is one inwardly (Rom 2:29).

The Heavenly Lover of the Canticles invites His spouse to the heights of Lebanon and Amana and Hermon, and there tells her to "look from the top." How different everything of earth looks when viewed from the place where one is seated with Christ in the heavenlies. "Behold, the nations are as a drop of a bucket, and are counted as the small dust of the balance. All nations before Him are as nothing, and they are counted to Him as less than nothing and vanity." When God says "all nations," He omits none. The school children of every nation are nurtured in national pride from the day they begin to read their history books; but national pride, like every other form of pride, is abomination in the sight of God. And pride of race must be one of the things that pass away when one becomes a new creature in Christ Jesus.

When seen from the heavenly viewpoint, how the present conflict is illumined. The policy of our God is plainly declared in the Word, "Peace on earth, good will toward men." The nations who have drawn the sword to kill those of the same blood in other nations, for God "hath made of one blood all nations of men," are not merely fighting against one another, but with their policy of "War on earth and ill will toward men," they are, without knowing it, again fulfilling the Scripture, "The Kings of the earth set themselves and the rulers take counsel together, against the Lord and against His anointed." Is any child of God going to side with these belligerent kings? Will he not rather side with the Prince of Peace under whose banner of love he has chosen to serve? The Kings of the earth strive for mastery and dominion, whilst He who sets in the heavens laughs and declares, "Yet have I set my king upon my holy hill of Zion." The Lord reigneth, though few have eyes to see Him. "The heavens do rule" (Dan 4:26). If these kings only had anointed eyes, they would cease their bloody conflict, and kneel in reverence to the King of kings who has given them a little power for a little space on earth, until He comes and takes the nations for His inheritance and the uttermost parts of the earth for His possession.

The nations of the earth have chosen the sword, and they who take the sword shall perish by the sword, even by the sword of Him who will come forth upon a white horse, clothed with a vesture dipped in blood, and His Name is called the Word of God (Rev 19:11–21). The world, especially the religious world, has no use for the children of God, but the Lord taketh pleasure in His people," and will let them share in His triumph over the nations. "Let the saints be joyful in glory . . . let the high praises of God be in their mouth and a two edged sword in their hands; to execute vengeance upon the nations and punishment upon the people; to bind their kings with chains, and their nobles with fetters of iron; to execute upon them the judgment written: this honor have all His saints" (Ps 149:4–9).

It is important for the saint of God to realise that his citizenship is in heaven, and that here he has no continuing city. The writer of Ecclesiastes sampled everything "under the sun" and he found it all "vanity and vexation of spirit." That is why the Apostle exhorts us to "seek those things that

"Our Heavenly Citizenship"

are above" and to set our affections on those things and not on things of the earth. We are told to bank our treasure in heaven, where thieves do not break through and steal, and rust and moth do not corrupt. Paul tells us that those "who mind earthly things" are enemies of the Cross of Christ. For himself, he declared to the Corinthians, "I determined not to know anything among you, save Jesus Christ and Him crucified."

There is a very practical side to this question also. I have noticed that many employers of labor in this country who have come from the old countries, choose for their employees men of their own nationality. Even though they become naturalized Americans, their love for their race predominates when it comes to preference in the matter of employing help in their various businesses. In these last days, the children of God are being crowded out from employment owing to their finding it impossible to become partakers of other men's sins, they cannot be party to evil business methods the world is adopting, many cannot conscientiously work seven days a week as many in the world want them to do, others again feel they cannot become members of trade unions, for they believe these to be a part of the organism of Anti-Christ. If employers of various nationalities give preference to their own fellow-countrymen, should not Christian employers give preference in the same way to those who are not only of the same "holy nation," but also sons of the same Heavenly Father? I know it is argued that the children of God are not usually so wise as the children of this world, and it does not pay to employ them. Yes, it may mean a few dollars less income but what after all pays best, a few extra dollars down here, or obedience to Him who tells us to do good to all men, especially to the household of faith. These are days when the children of God need to stand by one another in a very practical way. Having the same Father, are we not one family? Closer still, are we not members of the same body? Beloved, let us not love in word only, but in deed and in truth.[1]

---

1. Frodsham, "Our Heavenly Citizenship," 3.

17

"In the Last Days"

Frank Bartleman

1916

EVERYTHING THAT MAN HAS tried to do without God has proven a flat failure. And so with this present age. It has not turned out a "Golden Age." It is "dog eat dog" among the nations.

God hath "made of one blood all nations of men for to dwell on all the face of the earth, having determined their appointed seasons, and the bounds of their habitation" (Acts 17:26). They are denying His wisdom and justice in this and are seeking to "break their bands asunder" today (Ps 2:3). Hence wars, etc.

Man without God is to be feared always, as the author of all mischief, for the devil is back of him. He leaves a trail of misery and woe. No man is to be trusted without God. The spirit of national jealousy is at work. As the present war progresses it will be seen more and more clearly that the whole thing is a commercial struggle, on a scale such as the world has never known. A struggle for final supremacy.

The continuation of the present war, already long drawn out, shows clearly that it is judgement. There is no repentance in sight. No mention to quit fighting. Should a few more nations be drawn into it, which is very possible, ourselves included, it will soon resemble most closely the great wars prophesied for the end in Revelation. It is only a question of time when America must also come before God for judgement as a nation. Every honest man must know this. It may be our turn next. God knows.

The nations at war seem gradually to be settling down to wholesale killing as the normal order. This is terrible. The outlook is anything but assuring. There is no peace in sight. The world's conscience is being hardened. The milk of human kindness will run slowly. Great increase of cruelty is bound to follow this war. In fact violence is already greatly on the increase, even in our own land. A hardening is coming upon the people. This hardening of spirit is very evident to spiritual people. It is in the very atmosphere. Unnatural conditions abound everywhere. Trials and temptations are far greater than heretofore. It is the general hardness. God's Spirit is being driven out. The Gospel of love and grace has less attraction for the masses. They are no longer greatly appealed to. Selfishness and sin is dominant in them. "Lovers of pleasures more than lovers of God."

From a recent editorial in the Los Angeles Herald I have called the following lines from the pen of a distinguished psychologist: "I am in correspondence with scientific researchers in mind in many parts of the world. They write me of unusual mental states. Some fearful influence is agitating the lower faculties of the mind of man. I am alarmed over the thoughts there [missing word]." The Editor adds: "There is much to justify such an alarm. The crazy desperation and ferocious cruelties of the war in Europe, a slaughter pen of a magnitude unknown to previous human history, is enough in itself to discourage sane people.

Japan is hurriedly arming for some purpose. Even in American there is a vast increase in violence, explosions, homicides, suicides, and other horrifying things, often being only mere youths in age. All of these examples, and more, may well awaken fear among those who have been looking forward to the Golden Age and believing it to be close at hand. If it be true that some fearful influence is agitating the lower faculties of humanity—what is it? The conclusion the scientist first mentioned arrived at was that the mentality of mankind is now in a general abnormal paranoiac condition. That is letting the devil off easy.

In Germany there was a great harshness on the spirit of the people just before the war. Coming from gentle Sweden it seemed at first almost unbearable. And Satan seems also to be preparing the way for killing here. For two years our daily papers have been full of killing. Conscience is getting seared. A selfish spirit, refusing the voice of God, is predominating. God must give a rebellious people the sword.

Selfishness is overwhelming. There seems little interest even in the awful suffering and fate of Europe except for the dollars that can be made out of her distress. In fact there seems little feeling even for suffering in America. Monopolists are increasing prices in food stuffs, etc., against the common people. Fattening on their blood, taking advantage of their distress. They are human leeches. The rich man's dog gets more meat than the poor man's family. Great increase of crime must naturally follow increased want. Men grow desperate in their need, when their children are starving.

Our wheat is all being shipped to Europe. We have not nearly enough now to feed our own people in this country until next harvest. Two percent of the people are profiting by this marketing, while ninety-eight per cent are paying fancy prices, or going hungry. And the worst is yet to come along this line. Jas 5.

In a single week recently thirty-million dollars-worth of ammunition and shells was shipped from New York to the allies. Millions of men have been sent suddenly to account to their Maker in hot blood through this infernal trade of ours. Oceans of hatred unto murder have been stirred up. And shall we not also account for this? Has the dollar become almighty to us? Nothing must stop reason, humanity, principle, right, love, mercy, a pitying, pleading Savior, all must be trampled underfoot as long as we can make a dollar. We are creating seas of human misery, but we are gaining dollars. Is life given to make dollars, just dollars, at the expense of life and happiness, the groans and tears of outraged humanity, the murder of millions of men, and the sufferings of women and children? Must we have dollars?

This war has cost to date seventy-two-billion dollars. It is costing every hour four million dollars, to destroy men. The accumulations and savings of the entire world for fourteen years have been destroyed in two years. Fifty billion dollar's worth of property has been destroyed. Six million women and children have been made homeless. Tens of thousands have died of starvation. Four million have been killed. Eight million have been wounded. Three million, seven hundred thousand are missing. One hundred and twenty-five thousand square miles of territory has been laid waste. What raving madness!

The US Gov't Treasury and Assay Office holds today five hundred million dollars in gold. More than was ever gathered in one spot before since the world began. They say another year of war will free US of every dollar of indebtedness to any other country. No nation has ever held such a position in the world before. And this they call prosperity. But at what a cost! The jealousy of the whole world will be excited. That means war. And we are preparing. Not repenting. Nations seek God in times of adversity only. We are full of pride. Our trust is in defense, not God. We are not calling on God. "When Thy judgments are in the earth, the inhabitants of the world learn righteousness" (Isa 26:9).

"In the Last Days"

There are thirty million men in armed conflict with one another today. The effect of this on the spiritual atmosphere of the world is terrific for evil. "And because iniquity shall abound, the love of the many shall wax cold. But he that endureth to the end, the same shall be saved" (Matt 24:12, 13).[1]

---

1. Bartleman, "In the Last Days," 393–94.

18

"The World War"
Frank Bartleman
1916

GOD IS PUNISHING THE nations. England forced the opium traffic on China against her protest to enrich India at the mouth of the cannon, when China was struggling to save herself from death by legislating against the drug. England seized Hong Kong as her pay for China's resistance. At her door lies the responsibility for China's national curse.

A nation trained to sporting, running down poor little foxes with a regiment of men, women, horses, and dogs must make professional killers. Great meat eating nations make brutal people. England rules India with a handful of soldiers. The Indians eat no meat, and drink little alcoholic liquors. They are a mild people, but strongly intellectual.

Men are getting accustomed to bloodshed. One half of the world's population has been more or less effected with this spirit of hatred and murder. Man's boasted civilization, development in science, etc., has exploded in his hands. It is going to the scrap heap today. He has sought to save himself without God. But he has destroyed himself in his conceit instead. He cannot save himself without God. Man has abused his God.

Not long ago we were told we were to have wars no more. The reign of peace had come. And now they tell us the war is all for good, and that it is to work out the salvation of the race ultimately. What a change of front! Yea, what insanity! What raving! Willing dupes of the devil seemingly. The blaze of world war is beyond human control, sweeping all before it, like a huge prairie fire. Someone is going to have to answer for these millions of men, whose souls are being plunged untimely into eternity, in a death grapple of hate and murder with their equally unblameable fellow creatures of other nations. Millions have been despatched suddenly, all unprepared, at the orders of their rulers and leaders, their hands and souls dyed with another's blood. Oh, what surprise! How can they thus meet God? "Thou shalt not kill!" A worse than Herod has murdered these innocents.

And who shall answer for the untold suffering of armies and defenseless women and children, who have done no wrong? Even a Nero could rise up and condemn these rulers for a worse crime before God than even the burning of Rome. And every man that makes a dollar (even though it be an American dollar) out of the sea of human misery and suffering, is equally guilty and answerable before God. The word comes to us that our Mexican trouble has been settled, by request of the European powers, in order that the stream of American horses, ammunition, etc., may not be diminished in their shipment across the water. Who is to answer for the crime against the brute creation in this world war? For the using up of horse flesh? Oh, the multitudes of these poor, innocent creatures shot to pieces, left to die on the battlefield. Oh, the suffering from wounds and thirst, without attention, of these poor dumb beasts, man's best friends, and yet now creatures of man's coldest cruelty. Oh, God of heaven! How long wilt Thou bear with man! How long until Thy fury shall rebuke man's fury? "Now consider this, ye that forget God, lest I tear you in pieces, and there be none to deliver." Ps. 50:22. Over one million horses have been shipped to Europe for use in this war from the United States up to July 1916. "The earnest expectation of the creation waiteth for the revealing of the sons of God. The whole creation groaneth and travaileth in pain together until now" (Rom 8:19, 22).

Living is increasing in cost continually, through the shipment of our produce to the war countries, at fancy prices. Thus the rich are getting richer rapidly, and the poor poorer. This was England's curse before the war. The common people may rise up ultimately, as they did in the French revolution when the burden gets too heavy to be borne. Patience bears long. But when strained to the breaking point flies backward in proportion, sweeping all before it through the fury of a long suffering people. The trouble is not with the country or with the flag. God has given us these. But the abuse lies with the men in the positions of power.

Another curse of America is her graft, spendthrift habits, unsound business principles etc. The common people are exploited in the interest of the few. Prices must be kept up, though the people starve. The monopolist gets the profit, not the producer. This is bound to create internal disturbance, and will ultimately destroy any nation. Americans have not learned to economize as Europeans have. And they must answer for it. The cost of living has just about doubled in the last fifteen years in America. Yet each year there is destroyed in the United States four hundred million dollars worth of poultry and eggs alone. Comparatively the same money loss is true of every other product of the farm. And all because the merchants will not unload the supply on the markets for the benefit of the people. The quantity produced would bring the price down. They prefer to let it rot. Will God not curse for this? He will. It is a terrible crime. We are robbed of the food God has given us. Foreign interests in Wall St., are selling us out to the highest foreign bidder. And capital is enforcing militarism, against labor.[1]

---

1. Bartleman, "The World War," 296–97.

19

"Loyalty and Perseverance"
Ambrose Jessup Tomlinson
1916

THERE IS SURELY NOTHING more beautiful than real loyalty to Christ. It is counted patriotic for one to be loyal to his country. It is surely more than patriotism for one to be loyal to our Lord and King.

One may love his country and be obedient to its laws, and love it so well that he will die on the battlefield in its defense, and still be disloyal to God. And on the other hand one may be loyal to Christ and be disloyal to his country, because the laws of the county often conflict with the laws of Christ (Acts 4:19; 5:29).

When this is found to be the case, then it becomes our part to decide which of the two we will obey. Then we have to decide whether we will be loyal to Christ and break the laws of the country, or obey the laws of the country and be disloyal to Christ.

There was a law made to force all the people in the realm of [Nebuchadnezzar] to worship the golden image the king had set up, but there were three men that bluntly refused to do this because to do so would make them disloyal to God. They could submit to the penalty and suffer, but they determined to be true to God.

It means much to be loyal to our Christ now in this country in the face of some of the laws that have been made [Espionage and Seditions Acts], but no doubt it will mean much more a few years hence. Already some of our people are occasionally intimidated so they submit to some things that render them (shall I say?) disloyal to Christ and the Bible.

I wonder what such people will do when the laws are made still more stringent, and still more abruptly conflict with the laws of Christ. I suppose they will give up the service to the Lord entirely. If Peter and John,

Daniel and the three that were commanded to worship the golden image, had submitted to the decrees made by the legal authorities the countries, their names would not be held in holy reverence and high esteem as we see them today. If they had submitted, their names would have gone down in disgrace by the side of Judas and the many others that brought disgrace upon the worthy name they had previously professed to reverence and love.

The laws of Christ are given us to follow and obey or they are nothing. If they are nothing, then why were they given? If Christ gave us no laws, then what is He to us? If He gave us laws and we fail to obey them, what hope do we have in Him? (Luke 6:46.) What advantage is it to us to claim Him as our Savior, if He gave us laws and then we break and abuse them? How can we expect Him to stand for us if we fail to stand for Him?

What was it that won the favor of God for the prophet Daniel so that He should send him special word that he was a man greatly beloved? (Dan 9:23, 10:11, 19) It was his loyalty to God when he was forced to a decision as to whether he would obey God or man. What was it that gave Peter and John such great favor with God? It was suffering stripes and imprisonments rather than submission to the laws of the country that were contrary to Christ's laws.

I would not for one moment encourage law-breaking, but when the laws conflict with the laws of Christ it is up to [us to] decide which we will obey. And I am giving some example of those that remained loyal to God in preference to submitting to the laws of the country in which they lived. But they did submit to the country officials and suffered the penalty, so they could not be branded as traitors and insurrectionists.

Now if we are going to be loyal to Christ, it will require some perseverance on our part the same as it did for those that stood the test in former years.

Daniel purposed in his heart that he would not defile himself by obeying the king that would make him disloyal to God. And he persisted in following that principle till it landed him in the den of lions. But what did he care for that? It was his business to persist in loyalty to God no matter what were the consequences. So it is our business to be loyal to our Christ and His laws regardless of the consequences. The Bible is just like it is, and we should follow it closely.[1]

---

[1] Tomlinson, "Loyalty and Perseverance," 1, 4.

20

"The Christian and War: Is It Too Late?" [Part 1]

Samuel Booth-Clibborn

1917

No! It's not yet too late for us Christians to consider our relation to the war question. Yes! It is too late for the pacifists: for their weapons, being merely political, have failed, as everything human is bound to fail.

Yes! and the Socialists have failed too, having repeatedly scorned and rejected true Christian standards for those of a stupid and godless materialism. True, we have admired their devotion and zeal for peace. For the last two tragic years their burning enthusiasm (in America at least) has put us poor sleepy (though "professed") followers of the Prince of Peace to shame! But they are now bidden to "forever hold their peace," and that's the only brand of "peace" they are allowed to hold on to: for whatever is not build on "Christ the solid rock" is left to the fate of "sinking sand."

But what about us? Yes, us Christians, who have been preaching the gospel of love, joy, and peace so loud and so long? Now that is has come to practicing what we preach, now that the fiery test will be applied, are we willing to go through with Jesus? Are we ready to "go forth therefore unto him without the camp, bearing his reproach?" (Heb. 13:13)

Should a Christian Fight?

Let us examine carefully and prayerfully the principles of our holy faith, which principles we but yesterday rattled off so glibly, but which now means so much!

The subject is so vast and the space allowed so small that I shall confine myself to answering some of the popular objections to Christian nonresistance. However, be it clearly understood that the matter is treated from Christian standpoint only, and addressed only to Christians, the arguments being based solely on the authority of God's Holy Word!

Question: If war is wrong for the Christian, why did God himself in the Old Testament lead Israel into battle and into victory against their enemies?

Answer: The Jews were then living in the age of the law and judgment: while we dwell in the dispensation of grace and mercy! Right here is where there is an appalling amount of thick ignorance among God's own people, resulting in this everlasting muddling up of Old Testament and New Testament teaching of law and grace, of judgment and mercy, of war and peace, all through failing to "rightly divide the word of truth." We find recorded in the 17th verse of the first chapter of John's Gospel that "the law was given to Moses, but grace and truth came by Jesus Christ." God ordered Israel to wipe out in direct judgment the morally rotten Canaanites: but find me in the New Testament where Christ ever sent his followers on such a mission? On the contrary he sent them out to save men—not to butcher them like cattle. Again Jehovah openly declared himself on Israel's side, by starting miracles, both at Jericho and with Gideon, as well as at many other times and places. What nation now in the bloody mess can produce such proofs of its being in the right, or of God being on its side?

No! as far as the Christian is concerned, the "eye for an eye" system has given place to "turn the other cheek also" of Matthew 5:39-44. The reader is urged here to compare the following passages in order to realize the wide difference existing between Israel and the church of Christ:

ISRAEL	CHURCH
Difference in Calling	
Gen 12:1	Phil 3:20
Difference in Conduct	
Deut 7:1, 2	Matt 5:38–44
Difference in Worship	
Lev 17:8, 9	Matt 18:20

"The Christian and War: Is It Too Late?" [Part 1]

Question: Oh, it's all very well in theory, but suppose a brute in human form attacked your wife and children. Would you stand by and allow it? Having fired this broadside the patriot awaits the answer with an air of triumphant finality, while I'm supposed to rush blindly into the favorite trap. But praise God, he who is in the habit of receiving "tips" from heaven soon gets wise to such tricks; and now is for the answer.

Answer: In the first place the illustration does not fit the case at all, for the murderous individual tries to assault my family of his own free will, whereas in the war poor harmless people are driven like cattle and quite against their will by godless governments into butchering each other. A more fitting picture of the situation would be found in a Spanish-American cock-fight, where the poor benighted birds scatter each other's blood and feathers at their owners' pleasure—these latter together with the "neutral" spectators reaping all the profits.

In the second place, to substitute facts for wild supposition, thousands of humble Christian homes have never yet been broken into by a criminal of any sort: God protecting his own according to their faith; for they put their trust in him rather than in the police.

Third, if it should come to actual violence—Matthew 5 and Romans 12 would still remain true, and God's Word would still have to be obeyed (cf. the case of the three Hebrew children, Dan 3:16–23).

Of course I have not included the many religious persecutions which down the ages have been the inevitable accompaniment of every new and powerful movement: and yet these very persecutions have set the seal of God's approval in the most striking way on the doctrine of Christian non-resistance. Those early non-resisters, mind you, were the same martyrs, of whom, in these days of inherited religion, the boast is so often heard that "their blood was the seed of the church." Their sublime endurance under the most exquisite sufferings should not only draw pears from stones, but silence forever our contemptible excuses for crawling cowardice.

"And he said to me, These are they which come out of great tribulation . . . therefore are they before the throne of God . . . They shall hunger no more, neither thirst any more . . . For the lamb which is in the midst of the throne shall feed them, and shall lead them unto living fountains of waters: and God shall wipe away all the tears from their eyes" (Rev 7:14–17).[1]

---

1. Booth-Clibborn, "The Christian and War: Is It Too Late?," 5.

21

"The Christian and War: Christ Cleansing the Temple" [Part 2]

Samuel Booth-Clibborn

1917

Question: But didn't Jesus use force in a righteous cause when He drove the money-changers out of the Temple?

Answer: Yes, our Lord did use force. But what kind of force did He use? That is the crucial point of the whole argument! We shall therefore turn in calm confidence to God's own holy Word, in which alone we can find the eternal solution to this and other soul-piercing problems. It is also essential that we bring unprejudiced, humble, and earnest minds and hearts to bear on this matter, as I've found ninety percent of militaristic Christians to be lacking in the above kind of "preparedness,"—as is evidenced by a biased, feverish state of mind, fatal to clear spiritual thinking.

Twice did our Lord cleanse the Temple. Scholars usually divide His ministry into three "Passover" years. (See Dr. Robertson's "Harmony of the Gospels.") The cleanings recorded in John 2:19 signalized the first Passover of His ministry. The second occasion, of which we have the account in Matt 21:12, Mark 11:15, and Luke 19:45, took place three years later, during that last and fateful Passover of His Passion. The fact that there were two cleansings, far from weakening the argument, serves rather to confirm our position, by showing that His policy and principles were the same throughout.

Shall we then turn to John 2:13 (Revised Version)—"And the Passover of the Jews was at hand, and Jesus went up to Jerusalem and He found in the Temple those who sold oxen and sheep and doves, and the changers of money sitting—now let us carefully note every word—"And He made a scourge of small cords (Gk., whip of little strings) and cast all out of the Temple"—Who did He cast out?—"both the sheep and the oxen"—But didn't He whip the money changes as well?—let us read on. "And He poured

"The Christian and War: Christ Cleansing the Temple" [Part 2]

out the changers' money and overthrew their tables; and to them that sold doves He said: Take these things hence."

So we see that—contrary to popular opinion—the Word does not state that Christ whipped the men out of the temple; but only that He used the little whip on the cattle, for which it was naturally intended. The popularity of an opinion is no proof of its correctness. That it is now the fashion for Christians to go to war, by no means proves that God wants them to go.

Now, what arrests and compels attention in this episode, is the extraordinary and overmastering exhibition of divine authority and purely spiritual force, in comparison with which the mere chasing of cattle and overturning of a few tables sinks into insignificance.

Spiritual power—not carnal brute force—is the weighty fact we must grasp here. In order to a better understanding we must picture to ourselves the whole scene. A poor, humble, practically unknown man of the laboring class suddenly enters the outer Temple court, just as business is humming nicely; and promptly creates havoc! The frightened cattle rush out. The still more frightened owners gasp in bewilderment. "Grab the fanatic," cries one. "How dare he interfere with honest Passover business?" whispers another old hypocrite. And that's all. They all stand transfixed and helpless! Why? Ah, beloved, here's the secret, and may God help us to learn it!

There was something in Him that just there and then made them limp and helpless as infants. It was simply God's Holy Ghost power!

If we now turn to Mark 11:15-18, we shall see the same scene being re-enacted three years later; with only the difference that here the details are less prominent. Still the effect is just as sudden and as strange. The idea that He actually pushed the great crowd of men out of the Temple by physical force, is absurd, seeing that they could easily have overpowered Him. No, He just "began to cast out," and they went out. ("Being convicted by their own conscience," John 8:9.) His Word was enough. In v. 18, the chief priests tried to "destroy Him," but were likewise helpless.

Question: Well, but why did He use the Spiritual force in judgment rather than in mercy as on other occasions?

Answer: This pertinent query cannot be satisfactorily answered unless we bear in mind Dispensational Truth, that true key to the Scriptures. The whole of Christ's life constituted an overlapping period,—namely a period when the parallel dying off of the Old and germination of the New Dispensation were simultaneously going on. Thus Christ, while bringing in and formulating the new regime, not only had to fulfill most of the O.T.

prophecies concerning Himself, but also had to complete, and wind up—"pack-and-put-away"—the entire Mosaic order of things.

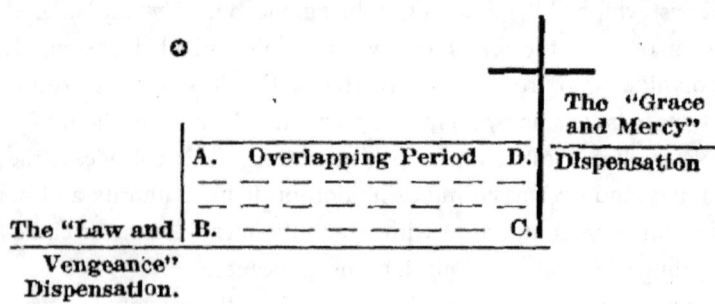

The "Law" age ends at the cross on the sketch. (C), with the rending of the veil, and the cry "It is finished." At [A] begins the age of "Grace and Glory," with the Bethlehem Star. So the whole figure (A) (B) (C) (D) represents the Overlapping Period. During this period, Jesus performed a yet more difficult task, that of transferring many old types and shadows into the new realities. Our present case strikingly illustrates all these functions of our Lord.

Only by "cleansing" the temple on the lower plane of the Law (B.C., in figure) could He complete the chain of proofs of His Messiahship and Kingship—according to the Law and the Prophets. This He did by fulfilling the "Messiah" prophecy of Ps 69:9 (John 2:17) and maintaining the tradition of righteous kings of Israel, whose first duty on mounting the throne was so often to "cleanse," repair, and re-establish Temple worship. (See Hezekiah in 2 Chron 29:15.) So, in the two-fold capacity of Israel's rightful King and Messiah, He first purified the Temple on the lower plane, after which He lifted the whole Temple Idea into the realm of Grace and Salvation, where He Himself, together with us, became the New and Living Temple of God." To whom coming, as unto a living stone, disallowed indeed of men, but chosen of God, and precious, Ye also, as [living] stones, are built up a spiritual house, [a] holy priesthood, to offer up spiritual sacrifices, acceptable to God by Jesus Christ. Wherefore also, it is contained in the Scripture, Behold I lay in Zion a chief corner-stone, elect, precious: and he that believeth on him shall not be confounded (1 Pet 2:4–6).

This beautiful truth is graphically set forth in our first narrative "What sign showest thou unto us seeing thou doest these things?"—drawing the

"The Christian and War: Christ Cleansing the Temple" [Part 2]

remarkable answer "Destroy this temple and in three days I will raise it up!" "But He spake of the temple of His body." "When therefore He was raised from the dead, His disciples remembered." And may we too remember that the Temple is now spiritual, and doesn't need to be defended by force.

Could anything be more pitiable than the slaughter of thousands of gallant young Frenchmen in the vain attempt to save the old Roman Catholic cathedral of Rheims;—as though God dwelt there! No! beloved "The Lord of heaven and earth dwelleth not in temples made with hands." Nor is the young Christian called to spill blood in defense of God-forsaken churches and nations, with all their pomp and pride. To them Christ is saying, as to the Pharisees of old, "Behold your house is left unto you desolate!" (Matt 23:38)

But there is another way in which the Temple can be destroyed, viz., by dragging into it the present horrible hatred, pride, and bloody butchery! "Know ye not that ye are the Temple of God, and that the Spirit of God dwelleth in you? If any man destroy (R.V.) the Temple of God, Him shall God destroy!" (And, "all they that take the sword shall perish by the sword.") "For the Temple of God is holy, which Temple Ye are!" Yes "Ye"—all Christians, whether German, French, or English (1 Cor 3:16–17). Yes, brothers! I can hear you protesting; but Paul knew you would "make excuse," for he goes on—"Let no man deceive himself. If any man among you seemeth to be wise in this world let him become a fool, that he may be wise, for the wisdom of this world is foolishness with God" (1 Cor 3:18–19).[1]

---

1. Booth-Clibborn, "The Christian and War: Christ Cleansing the Temple," 4–5.

22

"The Spirit of the Age"

H. Musgrave Reade

1917

TODAY, PEOPLE ARE REPEATING the question that has doubtless been asked every and anon during past centuries, "Why does God allow this war?"

The war is the working out of the inevitable law of God's government, the law of sowing and reaping. What is sown, that shall be reaped. The nations have been sowing the wind, and now are reaping the whirlwind. Why should God interfere with the law of cause and effect?

The majority of those who ask, "Why does God allow the war?" are men and women who emphatically don't want God in their own lives. He would be an intrusion. They are careful to close their hearts to the Gospel, and mean to make the best of things apart from Christ. They are living illustrations of that word in the old Book, "The foolishness of man perverteth his way, and his heart fretteth against the Lord."

All unbelief is belief of a lie. Where the truth of God is rejected, untruth is bound to take its place in the heart. Where the fear of God is unknown, there false, soul-running ideals will find a home. Where the Bible is discarded, a godless philosophy will deceive and enslave the soul.

'Light obeyed increaseth light;
Light resisted bringeth night."

"Science, Falsely So Called."

Science is literally "knowledge," and used in its strictly literal sense, means the aggregate of human knowledge of things material. But what is called "modern science," by dealing largely with surmise, enters into the realm of philosophy; it takes in the conjectures of the human mind in its attempt to discover what is at the back of things material, and represents man's groping quest after the reason for the universe.

Now, a man need be neither a scientist nor a philosopher to be able to detect the chief features of this "science" of today. Any laymen who reads and observes realizes that it has gained a very high authority in the world. In fact, "Thus saith science" is with many an end of all controversy; and a man has only to say that "science" declares such and such a thing to be the case, and vast numbers accept the statement without hesitation. Having discarded the Bible, people pin their faith with touching confidence to what has come to be regarded as a counter authority to the Word of God. Even Edison said, "There are more frauds in modern science than anywhere else." And the believer will remember that he is expressly warned against "science falsely so called." The saved man refuses to say to science and speculation, "These be thy gods, O Israel!"

"Modern science" is essentially [godless] and is really another name for unbelief. "Natural laws" take the place of God and the creator is virtually ruled out of His own universe. Seeing that the heart of the unregenerate man is against God, there is little wonder that the world is so ready to welcome any philosophy which, by rejecting all accountability to a personal, almighty holy God, makes man responsible to no one but himself. The foundation of this modern cult is, "There is no God;" and hence it is the science of "fools," and the fool has said in his heart, "no God."

The believer will be aware that it is the great aim of the arch enemy of the human race to make man occupied with anything rather than the things of God. Men are ready enough to try to turn this world into a sort of godless Utopia, where they will be able to carry out their own wishes without regard to the Gospel of Christ. And so they will eagerly hail any philosophy or religion that will help them to feel that they have no use for the Saviour. Hence we see the great concealed purpose of "modern science" is to rob man of the deliverance from sin which is alone to be found in obedience to the Gospel of the Lord Jesus Christ.

"Nobody is afraid of God now, said Dr. Dale, of Birmingham, some years ago, in a tone of dismay. A holy, filial fear of God is the spring of all true liberty, but where the fear of the Lord has decayed the power of man and his governments and organizations becomes increasingly despotic. On the principle that the strong can do no wrong, it has become increasingly easy for those in power to make wrongdoing legal and compulsory. The cuckoo-cry is "Organization is the thing." The individual man counts for nothing: the "thing" is all that matters. Many have been made to feel the despotic tyranny of trade unions over the conscience of the individual, and cannot but see that this modern craze for putting the organization before the man is antagonistic to vital Christianity which always insists upon the eternal salvation of the individual soul before the material prosperity of the community. It is refreshing to call to mind the sturdy words of Bishop Hooper: "Christ's kingdom is a spiritual one. In that neither king nor pope may govern. Christ alone is the Governor of His Church, and only lawgiver."

Lord Hugh Cecil, in writing to The Church Times on April 1, 1916, said: "The spiritual source of the war is to be found in a spirit of idolatry. Mankind has suffered the prodigious miseries that the war has brought upon us mainly because human beings in general, have come to love their countries more than they ought to do—more than they love God and His laws. This is the great spiritual evil of our time, an immoderate patriotism which has set itself in the place of religion, and gives to the state an authority which ought only to be given to God."

The "national spirit" tends to make men see everything through a distorted medium, and is a great enemy to a healthy conscience towards God. (Conscience towards God is the only conscience acceptable to Christ). This world spirit—the same spirit as urged the Jewish patriots and religionists to hurry the Son of God to Calvary—has hurried even true believers into committing themselves, in a most solemn way, to a business which is out of accord with the mind of their Divine Master.

Hypnotized by the spirit, high-placed ecclesiastics on both sides have made the vindication of the national cause identical with triumph of the kingdom of God!

And national sectarianism is responsible for the sentimental blasphemy that death in battle saves the soul?

This evil spirit is first aroused, and then played upon by inflammatory articles in the unscrupulous press. The deliberate suppression of "the other side of the case" is repugnant to elementary honesty; and yet there are souls whose Bible is their pet newspaper, and imagine that what they read in the popular press of the country, where the accident of birth has put them, is an adequate or honest statement of the facts, "He that will lie for the good of the 'cause' will lie as to the case being good for which he lies." And today we see the phenomenon of each of the belligerent nations claiming to be morally in the right, and its enemy morally in the wrong, while their respective rulers denounce each other as transparent hypocrites!"

"The Spirit of the Age"

The story of the dying soldier of Napoleon I (the "Kaiser" of a hundred years ago) is well known. As the surgeon was probing amongst his shattered ribs for the fatal bullet, he summoned his remaining strength and exclaimed, "A little deeper and you will find that Emperor." "What splendid devotion!" says one. "What awful idolatry!" is the verdict of every God fearing man. For here was one who was giving to a man, who was one of the greatest criminals that ever defiled Europe, the place that should alone be given to God. Poor soldier! He died as he had lived—an idolator.

It has been remarked during the present war that after all, the only religion which the average Englishman ever took kindly to is patriotism. Man is not merely an animal. He feels his need of an ideal. God's ideal for man is Christianity; but Satan is using the national spirit as an ideal to displace God's.

What an appalling sight confronts men today. Having rejected the Gospel of Christ, Christendom has adopted a new religion, national sectarianism, which leads to—mutual slaughter! In this new religion the believer will see a scourge of the devil with which the arch-enemy is lashing apostate Christendom. And in men's readiness to be duped by this modern idolatry he will realise how easy it will be for Christendom shortly to believe what is known in the New Testament as "the lie" relating to the antichrist, in the last days towards which the world is fast approaching. Satan's motto in regard to man is "*deceive* him: and *kill* him!" And who can deny that the great adversary is successful?

It is a remarkable phenomenon that each of the belligerent nations claims to be fighting for an ethical ideal superior to that of its enemy—a belief that makes the "will to slaughter" by each of the combatants all the more determined. In this way the great deceiver and murderer seeks to conceal the sordid beastliness of the battlefield. Here again the man of Christian intelligence will perceive the workings of awful satanic forces which are at work behind the scenes of the European tragedy. That things are no worse is largely due to God's despised people, who are engaged in "prayer warfare," and who are thus rendering an incalculable through unrecognized service to the world.

There are some who say that this war will end war. What a pathetic delusion! As if Satan would cast out Satan! "There are some," said a prominent Englishman, "who cherish the hope that out of the war will come a peaceful federation which will be enabled to secure peace on every occasion by mobilizing its forces against the disturbers. I regard that as a dream." War is a game from which all parties rise the losers. Life will continue dearer, and the unrest and discontent that marked the years previous to the great outbreak will probably be increased. Men will probably never come back again to normal conditions.

In recent years it was the fashion to boast in "the onward march of the human spirit." The world had its hope, and any who were bold enough to try to prick the bubble were scorned as fools and pessimists. That hope was that man was improving, that by process of evolution the human race was surely rising to a higher plane where the brotherhood of man would be universally acknowledged. But now this vain hope has been dashed to the ground. And yet the world never learns by experience along this line, and is busy building other hopes which must in turn be crushed. And although writhing in its miseries, it is still, wherever possible, whirling in its godless pleasures. It is blind to the fact that the godless "human spirit" which was its boast and confidence is the very cause of the European tragedy. And it is worthy of notice that the nation which above all glorified in its scientific knowledge, its culture, and its organized civilization is the very nation which has given the most appalling display of the worst passions of the human heart. No amount of civilization, science, or culture, can change the human heart.

The world's hope is a delusion. And why? Because it rests on a false foundation. Man's hope rests on man, and man is himself ruined by sin. The condition of the unsaved man is described in the Word of God in one short, decisive sentence, "Having no hope."

The Person of Christ is unique. He is "God manifest in flesh"; "the Way, the Truth, and the Life"; "the Light of the world." He promises rest of mind and conscience and heart to all who come to Him. He robs death its sting. To those who love Him the future is no longer a dismal gulf into which they fear to fall, and which they strive to forget, but is bright with hopes of home and glory. He is the sinner's friend; the only way back to God; the meeting-place between God and the soul. He is everything to the believer. His name is a strain of heavenly music. His titles spell perfection. In Him mercy and truth meet together. In Him are blended perfect truth and perfect grace; spotless holiness and tenderest compassion; absolute righteousness and boundless love; almighty power and infinite greatness. Reader, is He not worthy of your confidence?

He never angles for compliments. In royal, yet winsome tones, He commands obedience. Those who know and love Him as Saviour bow to

Him as Lord. He is the only competent Ruler the world can ever know. Unlike the world's rulers, He never debates what part of the truth to conceal in order to remain popular with His people. In Him there are no narrow limits of nationality, for He is the Son of man. He does not command His people to kill or be killed: He died Himself to save His people from their sins. Devotion to him does not involve injury to other men; on the contrary, His servants seek the eternal blessing of others. Unlike the world, He never deceives, and He always satisfies.

The believer will realise that all the nations from the same world. In spite of conflicting ambitions, all agree in rejecting the Lord Jesus Christ. There is no such thing as a Christian nation.

Let not the saved man waste his time and strength in making common cause with the world, and taking part in its godless schemes for political and social reform. A merely "reformed" person is just as really lost as is a criminal or outcast. The believer cannot alter the character and course of the world. Let him rather spend his strength in seeking to carry out God's eternal purpose of blessing towards men by projecting into the world the truth of the saving and keeping power of Christ, for "there is no wisdom, nor understanding, nor counsel against the Lord." The Gospel alone is the power of God for salvation. To succeed, as God counts succeeding, we must act along the lines of which He is working. Faithfulness to Christ is success: doing the will of God is usefulness. This is to be the attitude of the believer in a world whose attitude towards the Son of God is still, "We will not have this man to reign over us." True Christianity can never be popular. The believer is no longer a devotee of the spirit of the age. In contrast to the world's weapons of violence and fraud, he is to wield the forces of faith, and prayer and truth. He has renounced the idols of godless conscience, cultured unbelief and national sectarianism. He has rejected all "religion" save the religion of Jesus Christ. He has lost relish for the things for which the world toils and suffers and sins. And he should have no wish to identify himself with any of the world's "isms," but only with the full-orbed Gospel of the Lord Jesus Christ.[1]

---

1. Reade, "The Spirit of the Age," 13-15.

23

"The Awful World War"
Ambrose Jessup Tomlinson
1917

THE AWFUL WAR DEVIL is still slaying his millions. His greed and thirst for blood is never satisfied. He is agitating war on every hand. He is dragging millions of souls into his cruel grasp. Yea, he is slaying the young men in early life and breaking the hearts of millions of mothers and young wives.

Fond hopes of millions could have been blasted, and it seems that those in authority who could have some control, care for none of these things. They seem to value human life as nothing. Of course there is little thought about the souls and eternity.

Our country has kept out of the awful conflict so far. No doubt thousands of prayers have been underneath president Wilson and others in authority according to Paul's instructions: "I exhort therefore, that, first of all, supplications, prayers, intercessions, and giving of thanks, be made for all men; for kings, and for all that are in authority; that we may lead a quiet and peaceable life in all godliness and honesty. For this is good and acceptable in the sight of God our Savior; who will have all men to be saved, and to come unto the knowledge of the truth" (1 Tim. 2:1–4).

I admit that Jesus tells us that we will hear of wars and rumors of wars, but this is nothing new in the history of the world. Wars have checkered the history of the world in all ages. Different peoples have struggled for the mastery over others. All such result in bloodshed and the loss of human life. And what a waste of the lives of precious young men! And most of them probably died with no hope whatever in a Savior.

War is a feeder of hell. It increases the population of that dark region rapidly. This last awful struggle has been the cause of millions of mother's boys dropping into the region of the damned where they are entering their eternal tortures. Their fate is awful. And snatched away from life so suddenly by satan's belching cannons and the devil's war artillery, they had no time to repent.

With all the horrors of war vividly pictured before the people, and the shrieks and groans of the damned rightly imagined according to the teaching of the Bible, who favors war? Who would want to force a crowd of innocent young men into the face of death as he belches forth his hellish fury to hurl our young men off the battlefield into the fiery recesses of hell?

While Jesus said that there would be wars, there is no statement nor inference whatever that shows He endorsed or favored war. His teaching is altogether to the contrary. Better suffer wrong than to do wrong, is the spirit of Christ. At one time He said, "If my kingdom were of this world, then would my servants fight" (John 18:36). But as His kingdom is not of this world He teaches us to resist not evil (Matt 5:39), but rather if they smite you on one cheek turn the other also.

Our attitude toward war can be no other way than that taught by our Lord. If we are of the world so we can take part in the wars then we are not of His kingdom. We cannot be of the world and of the Lord at the same time. We cannot serve God and mammon (Matt 6:24). As for me I cannot fight Germany, nor lend my influence in that direction and support such a movement. I can be imposed upon, but I cannot fight.

No doubt many of our people are wondering what to do in case our country gets into war. Shall we enlist in the governmental service and fight for our rights? Can we shoulder a gun and march out to the battle front and point our gun toward our enemy and fire into his ranks and send his soul to hell, when Jesus, our King, tells us to love our enemies? (Matt 5:44)

There is scarcely any use for me to instruct our people about going to war, because the Holy Ghost, if given perfect right of way, will teach every soul to have the spirit of the Master. And it is plainly shown in the Book that it is not the spirit of the Master to fight.

Jesus loves the world. This takes in Germany as well as America. If we are Christ's, then we love the world too, and our love is not limited to our own native country. If Jesus fought because His rights were trampled upon, then we should do the same. But where do we see Him slaying the multitudes because they were trampling upon His rights? It is pride and selfishness usually that leads to war.

It is not my purpose to discuss war from the world standpoint. It is only my part to show that that Lord's children are citizens of another country. "Not of the world," says Jesus, "even as I am not of the world" (John

17:16). "For our citizenship (R.V.) is in heaven" (Phil 3:20). The war in which we are engaged is of far more importance than the world wars being waged. Ours is a spiritual warfare that seeks to save souls from hell instead of sending them there by flashing steel into their vitals.

Men are leaving their homes and loved ones and volunteering their service for their country and never return to tell them goodby [sic] before sinking into death. They call it bravery and patriotism to face the guns and bursting shells, but beloved, with us, it will be far more brave to excuse ourselves and stay in our own war that is far more important. The time may come when it will take stout hearts to refuse to shoulder a gun and march out to kill men. Many conscientious men have refused to carry guns under any circumstances. They felt it was contrary to the spirit of their Lord.

But we are too busy with our great work to stop and take a hand with the world. Our work must go on whether anything else is done or not. We can't stoop to accept a position lower than the one we already hold. Neither can we afford to work for less wages, which we have to accept if we leave our war and engage in the world war.

If war is declared on our country, much pressure will be brought to bear to influence our young men to volunteer. Enthusiasm will run high. The appeal to arms to support our country will catch like wild fire. Nobody will want to be called a coward at such a time and away they will go, and alas many, many, will never return. It may be easy for our own church boys to be caught by the spell. We must have them prepared to say, no, and stay as far away from the influence as possible.

We need our young men in the Lord's service. While they are so they can give the Lord the best of their lives is when they are most needed. What a sad thing to see a young life wasted in sin! Just as well say, what a sad thing to see a young man give his strength and manhood to send men to hell in bloody war, when he ought to be giving the best of his life to the active service of the Lord in building up the great Church of God.

Young men, let me appeal to you now! If you can leave home and go to war and travel over this world, no one knows where, and probably never return to greet your dear old fathers and mothers, or young wives with whom you are living so happily now, how much more can you afford to leave your homes to go to battle for the Lord and do your uttermost to save men from a devil's hell.

"The Awful World War"

As members of the great Church of God we owe our first and best to God. Our first duty is to the church. We obligate to be loyal and true. This, then, is our first duty. The war demon may try to persuade you that your first duty is to the stars and stripes, but this is a delusion. And you should never permit the spell that catches the world to get a hold on you.

The inspiration and zeal of war that is brewing now should only be used by us to put forth greater effort and show forth more fiery zeal and energy to push the battle for the Lord. We are short of soldiers now. We have none to give up to fight in carnal wars. We rather need more to help us than to give up some of ours to help them. They will do enough on their line without our influence. We need to nestle down and give our attention to His call closer than ever. We need to become so engrossed in His service that our ears will scarcely hear the call of the world.

Just now I feel our people need to hide away a little deeper under the shadow of the Almighty (Ps 91:1). There is a sense in which we can be hid away with Christ in God (Col 3:3) and still be in full warfare with the devil and his forces. A deeper and more vivid consecration to God will be necessary for every child of God this year. Don't think of trying to bridge over this year on flower beds of ease. There is no time for ease now. The [tensions] of the nations are tightened almost to the highest pitch. As our work is more important, more urgent, we must tighten our [tensions] up to the very highest pitch and plunge in to win or die, and win if we do die.

I hope our ministers and workers will not say in their hearts, I'll work at my trade this year and next year I will give my time to the service of the Lord. Your service is needed this year. The battle is on now. It may be over next year comes, and then you will not be needed.

Better get your best service in this year, and if the Lord tarries do the same next year, but never procrastinate on the Lord's time. The deeper the consecration the more spiritual one is, the less of the world will he want, and the less he will participate in world affairs, whether it be pleasures, politics, or wars. And the greater will be his enthusiasm for the Lord's work and the more faith he will have while he is engaged in the Lord's service. Then go deeper and give the best of your life to God and His blessed service. It will pay. Only do it, and God will bless you.[1]

---

1. Tomlinson, "The Awful World War," 1.

24

"The Awful War Seems Near"
Ambrose Jessup Tomlinson
1917

It may be that war will have been declared between the United States of America and Germany before this message reaches its readers. But I am sure many prayers are being offered up just now for our rulers and those in authority that we may be kept at peace and have the privilege of living a peaceable and quite life (1 Tim. 2:1, 2).

But in spite of all the prayers and good desires for peace and good will to men, the inevitable seems about to burst in upon our nation with all its horrors and slaughter. Excitement and the spirit of patriotism is rising and running at a pretty high tide. Nobody knows what the final outcome will be.

War is butchery and contrary to the spirit of Christianity. We, as a nation, make a boast of being a Christian nation, but how little the spirit of Christianity prevails. We are a boastful, proud nation, running to many excesses, and spending much of our time in mere play. In order for God to answer the many prayers that are constantly ascending the hill of the Lord, He will have to bring about a state of humility that does not now exist, and how do we know but what this is to be accomplished, by passing us over into the power of satan for the destruction of our pride and haughtiness (1 Cor 5:5).

While the awful war seems near, the saints of God should still remember that they are not of this world even as their Lord was not of the world (John 17:16). Our citizenship is not here, but in heaven (Phil 3:20). Jesus said if His kingdom was of this world His servants would fight, but as it was not, there would be no fighting for the mastery (John 18:36). Therefore He was delivered over to His enemies and slain by them because He would not fight.

"The Awful War Seems Near"

Here is an example for us. If our Lord could submit to His enemies and be imposed upon by them rather than fight, where is the authority for us to flee to arms and engage in the wholesale slaughter of our enemies because they are trampling upon our rights?

Indeed we love our country, and hope for peace and prosperity, but to level our guns and mow down our enemies like grass and hasten their souls to hell is not the spirit of our Master. And we are to follow Him. He is our example and we must follow in His steps (1 Pet 1:21). We are now cowards, but we want to follow the example and teaching of our Lord. If He joined the army and fought for His country then we should do likewise. But as He did not do this, we cannot.

Yes, the awful war seems near, but we cannot fight in carnal warfare when Jesus taught differently, both by precept and example. We might go on the battlefield and care for the wounded and dying, and lend our assistance in the hospitals, and preach to the soldiers, but we cannot take a gun and kill and mangle our enemies, when Jesus commands us to love them and to do them good instead of evil (Matt 5:44).

No doubt many of the saints of God are perplexed about the war problem. They are wondering what is right for them to do in case war is declared. Then they look still farther on and wonder what they should do in case the war becomes so fierce and far-reaching that they will be forced into the service against their will. We have but one way to determine our course. What would Jesus do? Ask ourselves this question and study the life and character of our blessed Jesus and apply it to ourselves and the problem is solved. I cannot dictate to anyone in detail. Matters of great moment will have to be decided by the individual on the spur of the moment. The instructions of Jesus that were given to follow in case of being brought before magistrates and officers will be safe to follow in such cases: "And when they shall bring you * * * unto magistrates, and powers, take no thought how or what thing ye shall answer, or what ye shall say: For the Holy Ghost shall teach you in the same hour what ye ought to say" (Luke 12:11, 12). Every child of God needs to get so close to God and live so in His presence that he can have the assistance of the Holy Ghost in these perilous times.

There is one thing sure, we cannot fight, but just how or what to do when the crisis comes to the individual will have to be determined at the moment. But as it is the duty of the Holy Ghost to help us at such extreme moments, I fully believe He will stand by us and lend us the necessary help.

I am sure He will not forsake us at such a time if we live to please him until that particular moment.

There never has been a time when it was more necessary for God's people to live close to Him than now. There have been times of greater persecution than now, but now is the time for us to live in constant expectancy of our Lord's return to redeem us from awful tribulations that it seems are almost ready to burst forth with all the hellish fury of his satanic majesty. The coming of the Lord is drawing nigh; and this is an epoch the world has never known.

While the awful war is raging, and the nations are [vying] with each other and engaging in the wholesale slaughter of men, the church must shine and bless humanity regardless of the world war. As members of His church, this is our duty and glorious privilege. And we must bless people of other nations as well as our own. There can be no respecter of persons with us. Help one as well as another when opportunity affords was the spirit of Him who wore the seamless coat. "As we have therefore opportunity, let us do good unto all men," says Paul (Gal 6:10).

I love for people to become enthused when their enthusiasm and energy can be spent in the right manner. But the saints of God have no surplus enthusiasm and energy to spend in fighting Germany. We need to use all of such that we have, to spread the glorious gospel into all the world to tell them of good things that can be obtained through our Christ.

I warn our people against enthusiasm and excitement over the war. This is a time for us to keep cool and continue in our efforts to evangelize the world. If there are any advantages to be gained in this respect by the awful world war, then we must utilize them and make progress while others may be giving their attention more to the war. If others who profess religion want to give their time and attention to the war, let them go, but we should bend all our energies to the one thing undivided.

The secular newspapers are full of the spirit of the world and calculated to inflame the minds of the American people with patriotic zeal. If war is declared public speakers will soon be infesting our country to enthuse the war spirit into our young men to induce them to volunteer to fight for their country, but we must guard against such things as much as possible on account of our religion. We have already enlisted to fight in a spiritual warfare for our Great General and Chief Executive and we must not betray our trust.

"The Awful War Seems Near"

We cannot afford to forsake the work of the Lord to display our patriotic zeal and bravery in a war against people for whom Christ died the same as He did for us. While others may do this, we cannot. Our young men need to spend their energy and strength in planting the gospel among the Germans rather than killing them and thus sending their souls to hell. We may not be able to take the gospel to Germany just now, but we can go elsewhere and we trust the time will come before long when we can plant the Church of God on German soil.

I admit that there will be awful wars and blood shed, and so much that blood will flow down the valleys like rivers, but nowhere does that Scripture show that the saints of God shall engage in this awful carnage. The Lord is to fight our battles for us while we spread the glorious gospel of love and cheer to the benighted and darkened souls of men and women of earth.

The Church must shine and bless humanity regardless of the world war. Now is the time for the "black woman" of Solomon's Song to keep and prune the vineyards of others in almost absolute forgetfulness of self-interests (Song 1:5, 6). Now is the time for the daughter to forget her own people and abandon herself to the service of the king (Ps 45:10). Now is the time for the preparation for the great day of the Lord. The signs are so plain that we need not be in darkness nor in doubt about the time in which we are living.

When we know of this and how the time is so short, we cannot afford to idle away moments by taking an active hand in the world war, nor spend our strength and energies in that kind of service when we should spend and be spent for God and His beautiful Church. This is the time for the church to come forth by leaps and bounds and make herself felt in this dark world. She has been hidden for ages, but now she must come forth, assert and show her power, and shine. "Arise, shine for thy light is come, and the glory of the Lord is risen upon thee" (Isa 6:1.), means the Church of God. It means the Church of God now. Then as we are members and loyal to His service we can have a part in this wonderful blessedness.

Come on beloved, let us go into the battle in which we are engaged with a little more zeal, enthusiasm, and courage than ever, and continue the work God has given us to do, even if our country is enthralled with war.[1]

---

1. A. J. Tomlinson, "The Awful War Seems Near," 1.

25

"War Notice"

Ambrose Jessup Tomlinson

1917

WE HAVE BEEN GIVING, from time to time, some little scraps of information about the registration and conscript act in order to urge our men to keep a close watch out for news or information from the government, so they could be ready to file exemption claims. I earnestly hope that all are now very well informed about the matter so they will know just what to do. The information has been given in the public press along as the government has deemed proper to dispense it. If, however, there are any that are not thoroughly acquainted with their duties I advise that they secure the assistance of a friend or attorney upon whom they can depend, because this is a particular thing, and a flaw on account of a little ignorance of the proper steps to take may prove disastrous and send them to the war, and this we want to avoid. The principles of the Church of God are against war, and we cannot afford to have our consciences torn and bleeding on account of being forced into it if there is any way out of it. So far, our government is reasonable and does not show any disposition to bind our conscience by forcing us into war against our religious convictions. Under the head of exemptions there are six reasons given for exemption. Only one of these will apply to our people with probably few exceptions. Number 2 reads thus: that you are a regular or duly ordained minister of religion. If the proper proof is formed and it is done in the proper order this will exempt our ministers. This ought to include Bishops, Deacons, and Evangelists, but this may depend on the interpretation of the law or rules in the hands of the exemption board. We consider each of these orders as regular ministers, sent forth to preach, baptize and receive applicants into church membership.

Under the head of Claims for Discharge, there are more reasons given whereby we hope to save our men. The main ones to apply to us are as follows:

8. That you are a married man with a wife or child dependent upon you for support.
9. That you have a widowed mother dependent your labor for support.
10. That you have aged or infirm parents dependent upon your labor for support.
12. That you are a brother of an orphan child or children under 16 dependent on your labor for support.
13. That you are a member of any well-organized religious sect or organization and existent May 18, 1917, and whose then existing creed or principles forbade its members to participate in any war in any form and whose religious convictions are against war or participation therein in accordance with the creed or principles of said religious organization.

This last will certainly liberate our people entirely, for we have been non-resistant from the very beginning, and one of our principle teachings has been, "But whosoever shall smite thee on thy right cheek, turn to him the other also." This is shown in a leaflet that we can furnish anyone on application.

The only difficulty I see in this is the preparing and filing of the proof and affidavits before the local exemption boards. In this, great care should be taken on the part of the registrant to have every item in perfect order.

Here is where it may be best in some cases to secure the assistance of an attorney, or friend upon whom you can depend, if you are the least bit in doubt of your knowledge and ability to perform such legal duties.

The time to attend to these matters is now here. You have seven days from the time you are called to your local board for examination to file your claim for exemption or discharge. Then after you file this claim you have ten days to prepare proof.

When you file your claim for exemption or discharge you must call for and obtain the necessary forms from the local exemption board. There is much information that has not yet been given to the public by the government and it is necessary for every registrant to watch his local exemption board office for any additional information that might be to his interest in filing claims or preparing proof, or anything else.

In filing these claims, and, as a church as a whole, we want to be able to prove to the government that it is not a matter of cowardice or rebellion, but strictly a matter of conscience and religious principles that causes us to make appeal for exemption and discharge.

If any of our members should in any way advocate war, or try to persuade any of these registrants to go on to war, or urge or enthuse them into a desire to fight, such members will be considered disloyal to the Church and also to the Christ of the Bible, and a continuance of the same may lead to the necessary action under our laws and principles. Such as this, however, seems very unlikely, as it is our purpose to have only such as members that are truly loyal to the blessed Jesus.

If you find according to your instructions that you will need our assistance in making certain proof about the church and its principles, you have only to call on us by mail or write and we will do our best to furnish it on short notice. We hold ourselves in readiness to help our brothers in this time of peril any way that is in our power. And we have certain writings prepared that every one may need which we will furnish on application.

If there are more than one of these points named that applies to you, then you should use them. File a claim for every one that applies to you, and your local board will furnish you with certain forms for every different cause if you ask for them. Never "swear," but always "affirm" in making your affidavits before a notary public.

Some of our friends outside the church have already appealed to us for assistance, but much as it grieves our heart we are helpless to lend them any assistance now. It is too late now even to join the church with that object in view. Pentecostal people ought to have seen something of the value of the great Church of God a long time ago. For years we have been heralding the message far and wide and trying to show those with whom we come in contact with that the Church of God is a means of protection for God's children, in these last days, and permit me to say that this will be proven more and more as the great day approaches.

As time runs on, God reveals the mysteries more and more, and we must get more and more settled down to working order as is required for the last days, deeper in His grace and Spirit and more thoroughly settled and protected under His great government—The Church of God.[1]

---

1. Tomlinson, "War Notice," 3. We are assuming that since Tomlinson was the editor in this period, he wrote this unsigned piece.

26

"The Pentecostal Movement and the Conscription Law"

The Weekly Evangel

1917

FROM ITS VERY INCEPTION, the Pentecostal Movement has been a movement of evangelism, studiously avoiding any principles or actions which would thwart it in its great purpose. All the wings of the movement, which have grown out of the work that originated in the Southwestern States and the Pacific Coast are a unit in this respect.

From the very beginning, the movement has been characterized by Quaker principles. The laws of the Kingdom, laid down by our elder brother, Jesus Christ, in His Sermon on the Mount, have been unqualifiedly adopted, consequently the movement has found itself opposed to the spilling of the blood of any man, or of offering resistance to any aggression. Every branch of the movement, whether in the United States, Canada, Great Britain or Germany, has held to this principle. When the war first broke out in August of 1914, our Pentecostal brethren in Germany found themselves in a peculiar position. Some of those who were called to the colors responded, but many were court marshalled and shot because they heartily subscribed to the principles of non-resistance. Great Britain has been more humane. Some of our British brethren have been given non-combatant service, and none have been shot down because of their faith.

It has not been seriously considered that the General Council of the Assemblies of God (one of the prominent branches of the Pentecostal Movement in the United States) would find it necessary to interpret its attitude toward war, until the war clouds gathered and actual war was declared. Neither the General Council, nor any other wing of the movement that we know of, have ever written a creed, therefore it was found necessary for a number of the official members of the Executive Presbytery to assemble together and draw up a resolution interpreting the established principles or creed of all sections of the Pentecostal Movement, and especially that part represented by the General Council. A resolution was formulated, approved by the Executive and General Presbytery, and forwarded to President Wilson on April 28th, 1917. The letter to the President and the resolution were as follows:

> Resolution Concerning the Attitude of the General Council of the Assemblies of God Toward any Military Service which Involves the Actual Participation in the Destruction of Human Life.
>
> While recognizing Human Government as of Divine ordination and affirming our unswerving loyalty to the Government of the United States, nevertheless we are constrained to define our position with reference to the taking of human life.
>
> WHEREAS, in the Constitutional Resolution adopted at the Hot Springs General Council, April 1–10, 1914, we plainly declare the Holy Inspired Scriptures to be the all-sufficient rule of faith and practice, and
>
> WHEREAS the Scriptures deal plainly with the obligations and relations of humanity, setting forth the principles of "Peace on earth, good will toward men." (Luke 2:14); and
>
> WHEREAS we are followers of the Lord Jesus Christ, the Prince of Peace, believe in implicit obedience to the Divine commands and precepts which instruct us to "Follow peace with all men," (Heb. 12:14); "Thou shalt not kill," (Exod 20:13); "Resist not evil," (Matt. 5:39); "Love your enemies," (Matt. 5:44); etc., and
>
> WHEREAS these and other Scriptures have always been accepted and interpreted by our churches as prohibiting Christians from shedding blood or taking human life;
>
> THEREFORE we, as a body of Christians, while purposing to fulfill all the obligations of loyal citizenship, are nevertheless constrained to declare we cannot conscientiously participate in war and armed resistance which involves the actual destruction of human life, since this is contrary to our view of the clear teachings of the inspired Word of God, which is the sole basis of our faith.[1]

---

1. "The Pentecostal Movement and the Conscription Law," 6.

27

[Members Seeking Conscientious Objection]

C. H. Mason

1918

MY NAME IS C. H. Mason; I am General Overseer of the church of God in Christ. Along last summer I sent out the certificates of membership to the various pastors of my Church and the Overseers. A copy of the certificate of membership which was sent out to be issued to the members reads as follows:

Faith of the Church
of God in Christ
Born in the Mind
of its believers 1895

Its belief is in God the father, and Jesus Christ the Lord. Its creed is the New Testament, it holds for peace and good will toward all men as said in Heb. 12:14, which is as follows: Follow Peace with all men and Holiness, without which no man shall see the Lord. It believes in true Holiness unto God. Ephesians 4:22.

The members of said church are not allowed to carry arms, to shed the blood of any man, and still be members of said church. Scriptures that forbid them in their creed: Matt 5:38–42: there the Lord says resist not evil (Rom 12:17; 1 Thess 5:15; Heb 10:30). Vengeance belongs to God. Whoso sheddeth man's blood, by man shall his blood be shed (Gen 9:6, Rev 13:10).[1]

---

1. Quoted in Beaman and Pipkin, *Pentecostal and Holiness Statements on War and Peace*, 156–57. This statement was sent by C. H. Mason to Church of God in Christ leaders in July 1917 to give members seeking conscientious objector status to be given to the draft board. The form was entered in testimony from C. H. Mason at trial in Austin, Texas, in 1918. C. H. Mason's testimony dates the document transcribed here as

28

"Days of Perplexity"

Ambrose Jessup Tomlinson

1918

With the commotion that is now in the world it seems an easy matter to see that this is the very time referred to by Jesus when He said, "And there shall be signs in the sun, and in the moon, and in the stars, and upon the earth distress of nations, with perplexity; the sea and the waves roaring."

There is great distress on every hand and in all the world. Previous to this time there have been times of local distress, but this is a time when it is universal. Every nation is more or less affected. Every home, rich and poor alike, is touched by the influences of the distress to a marked degree.

Whole nations are distressed. They do not deny it. Destruction, want, poverty, misery, and everything that it takes to fill the measure of the meaning of the word. Along with the distress of nations comes perplexity. Jesus said with perplexity. People of all classes are in a state of bewilderment. This means the days of perplexity have come.

While the people of the world are perplexed, this spirit of perplexity has also taken hold of many good people. They do not know what to do. They are anxious to do the very right thing, and will do it faithfully if they know it, but they do not know, hence they are perplexed.

This war draft law, and the war itself, are giving our people much concern. We cannot fight and we are sometimes at a loss to know just where to draw the line. We are helping in the war by paying high prices for food and clothing, but these are necessities and we cannot refuse to purchase them.

We are helping in the war by using the mails purchasing postage stamps, but we cannot stop our correspondence. We are helping in the war by borrowing money at banks and purchasing revenue stamps, but many of our people are in debt and are compelled to get small loans occasionally.

---

originating the previous summer, 1917.

"Days of Perplexity"

We are helping in the war when we work in the coal mines and dig coal for the government or for companies. The farmer and truck grower, the merchant and mechanic are not exempt from assisting in the war. It makes scarcely any difference what one engages in now he is helping in the war more or less in some way.

Contributions to the Red Cross, or to send aid to the soldiers, or purchasing liberty loan bonds, or doing service of any kind and in almost any manner is assisting in the war directly or indirectly.

But we say we cannot kill; this is true, and yet indirectly we are lending our assistance in the very thing our conscience condemns. We are helping to pull the triggers that fire the guns that take the lives of our fellowmen. We do not want to do this, but it is forced upon us. Our people know of all this and they are perplexed about it, and they want to know what to do about it.

Our evangelists and ministers feel the message of love burning in their souls, and are hurrying to carry the glad news by traveling on the railroads, are aware of the fact that they are aiding the war by paying the extra tax for tickets. They are seeking to save the lost in one place and helping to destroy and kill in another. They go on a mission of love to bless, but by paying their train faire they help to curse. They are hurrying to keep souls out of hell, and pay a tax that is used to help send souls to hell.

There is no use trying to deny this, it is too true. But it is in our hearts to bless and curse not (Rom 12:14). We do not want to kill and mangle our fellowmen, and we do not intend to do it directly, but we are lending our assistance in this matter perhaps in a thousand ways.

I know our people are greatly perplexed about this matter, judging by the hundreds of letters that are pouring into our office every week. I suppose we have answered thousands of questions since the enactment of the war draft law last May. There have been times we have been compelled to give the war question more of our valuable time than the beloved Church. This is a grief to us, but it has to be done. We are bent on doing all we can to assist our people in this matter. But we have neglected other work to attend to this class of work. I feel pressed to repeat: These are the days of perplexity.

We have succeeded in getting some of our men exempt from the firing line, but it places them in other positions that aid the war, and this cannot be avoided unless we decide to refuse to serve the government in any line and take the consequences. Then to do this it would be difficult to draw the line and know just where to stop.

Now is a time when the greatest wisdom is needed. I am sure that there are thousands of prayers offered for the general overseer every day. They are asking God to give him wisdom and ability to meet the requirements under all circumstances. They are anxious for him to be able for every emergency, and he feels the effects of their prayers as he prepares his official appeals to the government. Just as this time important matters are under consideration. Earnest prayers will turn the hearts of government officials. Much prayer is needed just now while we are swinging in the balance.

Under the present conditions it is no time for [frolicking] around and making hasty conclusions. Cool-headed deliberate decisions are necessary now. It is a good time now to apply the advice of Jesus given at Luke 11:2–32, and sit down and count the cost, and it is not so easy now to tell what the cost will be, but some people will pay the price and go through and reach heaven no matter what it is.

Some are afraid to accept too much and sign too many papers for the government for fear they will accept the mark of the beast, and they would die rather than do this knowingly. But they do not know, and this is cause for perplexity. The way we have to do to purchase fuel in the cities, and the war taxes and registrations all look frightful to our people who are conscientious and want to please the Lord. They do not want to submit to anything that will cause them to lose their souls.

It will be a pleasure to me to assist our loved ones in some way so they can go on with their work of spreading the gospel without too much perplexity. Our work is important and must be prosecuted to the end. The gospel must go and must travel rapidly and should be unhindered, but as Paul acknowledged that Satan hindered him, we are forced to acknowledge that Satan is hindering us now more or less. But we are mustering our forces and preparing to work harder this year than ever. And I believe we will accomplish more for God regardless of the war and all the perplexities that may appear.

There is one thing special to which I wish to call attention right here. When Jesus was asked, "Is it lawful to give tribute to Caesar, or not?" Jesus called for a penny. When they had brought it to Him "He saith unto them, whose is this image and superscription? And they said unto him, Caesar's. And Jesus answering said unto them, Render to Caesar the things that are Caesar's, and to God the things that are God's (Mark 12:15–16).

"Days of Perplexity"

By the above incident we believe Jesus furnishes us with a fair explanation of our duty under the present circumstances. The government requires certain taxes, so we will have to pay them where required in order to continue our work in spreading the gospel. We are not responsible for what the tax is used. When Jesus was required to pay tribute He did not ask for what purpose the tribute money was to be used, He only sent Peter out after a fish to get the money to pay it. If it had been used for war it would have been the same with Jesus. He was sending to Caesar the things that were Caesar's. This is the way we will have to do.

We do not approve of capital punishment for criminals, but we pay our tax and this helps to pay salaries to officers that execute the laws, one of which is to hang or electrocute certain criminals. War is a wholesale slaughter while hanging and electrocuting are only occasional, but the principle is the same.

I would not serve in an office where I would be compelled to take a life when the law said do it. I could not take a gun and fire it at my fellow men even at the command of a military officer. I could submit to the penalty inflicted upon me for refusing, but I cannot kill. I doubt if I could take the obligation to become a solder in the first place. I do not say that other[s] should not. There is a stopping place, but it may not be necessary for me to mark the line. If our men are forced into the fighting lines it will be considered by us as a mark of persecution. If our government wishes to lower its standard of freedom of conscience and attempt to compel us to fight when we refuse we cannot prevent it, but we will be obliged to enter the fact upon the pages of history as persecution if they inflict penalties upon us when we politely refuse to kill.

We are facing some very grave problems. We do not know the final results, but God is going to give us grace and wisdom. We are in the world, but not of the world. While we are here we must obey the laws of the country in which we live so long as those laws do not require us to disobey God, then God must be first even if the penalty is inflicted upon us. This is God's Word. Here is where we must stand. We must be loyal to God and to one another. We must stick close together now in these days of perplexity, and trust God to give us the necessary wisdom and love. I believe He will do it.

Surely, surely, we will put aside everything that has the least tendency to create friction or crosses between individuals, and stand firmly knit together in love. We must lovingly and tenderly bear with one another in our understanding. In speaking of one another to others we should use the most endearing terms, and when we talk together a good sweet spirit should always prevail.

I wish I could emphasize that sweet word "love," but I would much rather exalt the experience and the importance of having it in our lives. "Lover never faileth." We need something that will not fail now in these days of perplexity. Everything else may fail in these days of peril, but this one thing will stand. "And now abideth faith, hope, love, these three; but the greatest of these is love" (1 Cor 13:13).[1]

---

1. Tomlinson, "Days of Perplexity," 1.

29

"The Patriotic Harlot"
Elbert Carlton Backus
1918

THERE IS NO BETTER example of the inconsistency of churchianity in general than its attitude towards that which the world calls patriotism,—no better example of its morbid ideals and of its faulty interpretation of Christianity.

The common conception of patriotism is accepted by the church without question. And why not? For 1600 years it has been the one great moulder of human ideals. Now in what it is pleased to term the highly enlightened and civilized 20th century shall it begin to disown that which it has been hundreds of years in bringing to pass? The leopard may change his spots and water may turn and run up hill, but apostasism will never lose its characteristics. Never will it cease to point with pride to its achievements. Never will it cease to excuse and to defend its inconsistencies and its narrowness, nor to assert its holiness and infallibility. But even if the popular conception of patriotism had sprung from some other source and the church doubted its legitimacy ever so much, the conservative, suave, compromising, insidious proselyter would surely adhere to its age old custom of following the lines of least resistance, the broad road to good favor and wealth and force its conscience to yield before public opinion.

Church patriotism, like the church itself, is outwardly beautiful but inwardly full of dead men's bones and of all uncleanness. The idea of noble self-sacrifice stands out boldly, so boldly in fact that all the disgusting, inhuman things connected with his profession are forgotten, or ignored, and the ideal patriot is glorified as one who has stood the supreme test and has laid down his life for others,—for his country. Certainly such self-sacrifice, if prompted solely by Christian love, is sublimely beautiful and eminently Christlike; for "Greater love hath no man than this, that a man lay down his life for his friends." But let us pause just here to reflect that no love can possibly be Christian which is not universal in its scope. Christ loved ALL mankind, Christ died for ALL mankind, and although, in life, he was the champion of a great and just cause and waged a fierce warfare, when he at last was ushered roughly into the presence of the Father, not one drop of blood stained his hands save what was all his own. From the dying Christ and his compassionate prayer: "Father forgive them," turn to the uniformed idol of Christendom, sloshing heedlessly through the blood of his brethren, fighting like a demon until he himself is stricken; see HIS dying eyes burn with the bitter hatred of his soul even after his palsied hands refuse to move, and hear HIS last breath come hissing through clenched teeth, laden with a horrible curse upon the foe. Ah, who has failed to note that behind the beautiful veil of martyrdom covering church patriotism there lurks another idea so repellent that no soul untainted by the virus of hell could fail to turn shuddering away from the hateful thing. Who has failed to note the significant fact that the ordinary person does not think of patriotism apart from flags, marching soldiers, and the roar of battle. Who does not realize that the popular patriot in addition to all his seemingly good, Christ-like qualities must also be a murderer!

War is intensely barbarous; the favorite medium through which the demon of hate gluts its hellish appetite with tears, blood, and human carrion. Yet wars would not, could not be fought against the will of professed apostles of love and peace. The Williams, Georges, Nicholases and Wilsons together with most of their subjects and supporters are "Christians," at least, they are members of "God's" church, rulers by divine right, etc; yet they have rushed together, these brethren of God's family, in the most senseless and awful fratricidal butcheries the world has ever known. Then while these Christian rulers recklessly pour out the God given resources of earth and destroy the flower of the human race, think of the hundreds and thousands of flag decorated churches where the sanctimonious servants of the devil congregate on the holy Sabbath and offer up their sacrilegious prayers, beseeching the Prince of Peace to throw his influence and power into the balance on the side of Catholics, Methodists and Baptists who are trying to kill their brother Catholics, Methodists and Baptists who are so unfortunate as to live just across some imaginary national boundary line. Then think of these prayer mumbling, psalm singing hypocrites calling upon God with their next breath to bless the millions they are giving and the hundreds of missionaries they are sending to preach the gospel of Christ to the heathen. Oh, God!

"The Patriotic Harlot"

Falling heir, as we have, to the false teachings of the past and to their resulting false conceptions which have been drilled into and fastened upon us by every conceivable agency, it is hard for us to realize just what sort of world ours would be today, if instead of teaching patriotism, with its narrow clannishness, selfish nationalities and deadly strife the church had risen high enough in the scale of Christianity to at least teach the doctrine of the despised infidel who declared the world was his country and his religion was to do good. Certain it is that the earth, after so many centuries of such teaching, would not now be war torn as it is, and the church would not stand responsible, as it surely does, for the present world war and for numberless other wars which have [preceded].

Oh, the bloody harlot, Apostasism! Born just outside the Garden of Eden, and thriving today as never before upon the errors, inconsistencies and corruption of the modern church, it has never ceased since the days of Cain to follow off after its Baals, its Mohammeds, its Fathers and its Reverends; all the while offering up religiously its imperfect and unacceptable sacrifices to God. It has always been devilishly aggressive, this old harlot, compassing land and sea to make one proselyte, compromising, adulterating, nullifying and even forcibly suppressing genuine Christianity, substituting its filth[,] malice and hate for righteousness and love of the religion represented by Abel, Moses and the Christ.

The apostle, John, looking far down through the centuries to come saw apostasism with all its idolatrous sects of every description and denomination represented by a lewd woman, drunken upon the blood of those who loved the plain, pure truth. After the Philistine and the Jew, the Christian and the Mohammedan, the Catholic and the Protestant had all fought their "Holy Wars;" after the sanctified Methodists had returned the hate of the "grace" endowed Baptists; after false religion had done its perfect work and had set every man against every other man, and the world had become one seething mass of suspicion, enmity and strife, John saw the source of German "Kulture" and hell on earth.

The thing he saw was inconsistent churchdom; the American branch of which, as a Christian institution, had observed nationally a day of prayer for the cessation of human slaughter and then in a few months, as a patriotic institution, observed another day of prayer for bloody victory. The thing he saw was all false religion of all time which had deceived the nations and with which the war lords of earth had committed fornication. "And in her was found the blood of all that were slain upon the earth."[1]

---

1. Backus, "The Patriotic Harlot," 4–7. Backus was formerly a Methodist and a lay preacher for at least a year, but was removed a few years from the ministerial rolls. By 1918 he seems to have transitioned to a Pentecostal faith, loosely called "Holiness Mission," or "Holy Roller." It is possible that in transition from Methodist to Pentecostal he had espoused a form of socialism. Sometime later he returned to the Methodist Church. Backus and a close colleague, Lon Echols, led a congregation that met in a barn in Highland Park, Kentucky. Both were indicted by a US Grand Jury in Louisville, Kentucky in July 1918 for espionage, for this publication among others, and for their efforts to disrupt the war. The periodical states: "The paper [*The Comeouter*] has absolutely no financial support besides what the editors are able to furnish; and they are both poor men, dependent for a livelihood upon their daily labor" (7).

30

"Christian Citizenship"
Frank Bartleman
1919/1920

"For our citizenship is in heaven; from whence also we wait for a Savior (Deliverer), the Lord Jesus Christ" (Phil 3:20). "Now then we are ambassadors for Christ" (2 Cor 5:20; in a foreign country).

The warfare of the "Reds" against the church is the law of retribution, God's judgment on an apostate, fallen church. Judgment has "begun at the house of God." The "Reds," wicked as they are, God defying and Christ rejecting, are His scourge to punish an apostate church, and to break the wicked nations. They are preparing the way for Antichrist, the Lawless One. And that will bring the final judgments of God upon a Christ rejecting world.

Two great iron jaws are coming rapidly together. The Apostate church system, and Socialism. The true church will be caught and ground between the two. The Socialist system is distinctly antichrist. A true Christian certainly has no part in it. The Socialists class all Christians alike. They believe Christianity to be at the root of all world troubles. What a shrewd move on the part of the devil! With one sweep he would rid the world of Christ and Christianity. The autocratic, ruling, capitalistic classes have usurped church authority, using it to bind the consciences of the people. This the Socialists are determined to destroy. The system has proven a traitor, terribly misrepresenting the Gospel of our Lord Jesus Christ and the grace of God. The people have been deceived. Retribution follows.

And this is world politics. What place has a Christian in it? It is all corruption and hypocrisy, hopelessly fallen. "These shall hate the harlot and shall make her desolate and naked, and shall burn her utterly with fire. For God hath put in their hearts to fulfill His will" (Rev 17:16–17). This the "Reds" are fulfilling before our eyes. And it is heading this way. A pure, martyr church will be separated by this means, through persecution. Persecuted by both factions. Each would compel us to fight for them. So the move that paves the way for Antichrist also brings forth the "martyr" company.

John Wesley said, "Shall Christians assist the Prince of Hell, who was a murderer from the beginning, by telling the world of the benefit or need of war?"

As Christians we are "born again," this time into the Kingdom of God. We are citizens of the country we are born into. The Christian is a "man without a country," as far as earthly citizenship is concerned. He renounces his earthly citizenship in this world when converted, as surely as one renounces his citizenship in the US, should he swear allegiance to a foreign country. "Who hath delivered us from the power of darkness, and hath translated us into the Kingdom of His dear Son" (Col 1:13). Our "citizenship" is in heaven. Heaven is our country. We are to "render unto Caesar the things that are Caesar's." But our lives and souls belong to God. He gave them. We must "render unto God (not Caesar) the things that are God's." Caesar disputes this ownership with God.

A Christian has no more to do with the politics of this world than an American has with the politics of Europe. The church can only take part in politics when she is worldly. The early Christians were persecuted because they were Christians. They were not accorded a place in the world. They were not citizens here. And the world recognized the fact. They were different. This treatment kept the church clean. Only "new creatures" could bear the test and live under such persecution and hatred. "Because ye are not of the world, therefore the world hateth you" (John 15:19).

To go to war the church must go back under the Law. But the Church was never under the Law. Israel was under Law, in the Old Dispensation. The Church was born under Grace.

We are living in the "as in the days of Noah" time. The majority will be taken by surprise, all unprepared, as they were when the late World War broke forth. They were swept off their feet, into the dreadful maelstrom of hate and murder. How few will heed the warning! They are living in a "fool's paradise."

He who justifies the church in going to war under the Gospel, proves he knows absolutely nothing of the nature of the Gospel. This is the "foolishness of the Gospel." "Unto Gentiles foolishness." "For He was crucified through weakness. We also are weak in Him."

"Christian Citizenship"

The Gospel of Christ is "weakness" in the eyes of the world. It will not fight for its preservation, therefore it is despised and condemned utterly.

In times of war we are forbidden to preach the Gospel. One must preach murder, hate and revenge. The Gospel teaches "love your enemy, do good to them that hate you, and pray for them that despitefully use you." And "resist not evil." "Who, when He was reviled, reviled not again; when He suffered, threatened not; but committed himself to Him who judgeth righteously." What foolishness to the world! None but a real Christian can do this. "Love worketh no ill to his neighbor," but rather "doeth good unto all men." The Christian must obey the Gospel. We are bound to "obey God rather than men." Gov't [Government] is squarely up against God in its demands on Christians during war time. And Christians are squarely up against the question whether they shall obey God or man.

Should those in authority forbid the preaching or practicing of the Gospel, which Gospel forbids to the Christian the exercise of war, there is but one thing for him to do. He must obey God. Let human governments remember they also have One to whom they must account. They are subject to the King of kings and Lord of lords. Nations rise and fall at His word. Should an enemy appear, the Christian is bound to do only good to them. He must suffer the loss of all things, yea, even of life itself if need be, rather than "resist evil" by defending himself by carnal means to the intended injury of an enemy. This is the clear teaching of the Word. God can change the hardest heart in his favor. He can protect those who trust Him, for His glory. There is no other course for the Christian to pursue. He may not defend himself by violence. To do so, is to forfeit the protection of God. He is utterly defenseless, except for God.

Only the Christian's cause is righteous after all. The wicked are to be punished, on whatever side. The Christian is not to protect the wicked from the possible righteous judgment of God. "He that killeth with the sword must be killed with the sword. Here is the patience and the faith of the saints." Rev 13:10. How few accept the Gospel standard in such case. If we would prove God we should not need to defend ourselves, or others.

"The time of this ignorance God winked at (passed over), but now commandeth men everywhere to repent." Who would say that the issues in Washington and Lincoln's day might not have been settled without blood if those who named the name of Christ had but possessed the Spirit of Christ? Antichrist aims soon to control all government. Must Christians obey Antichrist? The church has lost the light of her early age. She has been "in the wilderness." But she is coming out. "Fair as the moon, clear as the sun, terrible as an army with banners," clothed with the power of God.

An apostate church goes to war with carnal weapons. But judgment follows. Having taken the sword, they perish with the sword, as the Scriptures hath said. It acts automatically. Zwingli went to war, and perished miserably on the field of battle, at Cappel. Christian rulers lost their thrones and lives in the late war. Our own President Wilson was paralyzed as a result of the great strain. Do we realize that "the whole world lieth in the wicked one?" And are we really seeking to be saved from "the world, the flesh, and the devil?"

Can we imagine Jesus or the Apostles going to war at the behest of the Roman government? Converting men by the power of the Gospel, and later killing these same converts, across some imaginary boundary line? Imagine Christian meeting Christian on the actual field of battle, and murdering one another. To a really converted man the idea is unthinkable. First Gospel, then bullets? How are the mighty fallen! War for what? Territory, commerce, etc., for the supremacy of one nation over another. Our Gospel is a Gospel of love, not hate and murder.

The Christian dare not obey even government decree when opposing the command of God to him. He must not seek to harm an enemy. He cannot engage in war under any circumstances without doing violence to the Spirit and command of Christ. The Gospel is "foolishness" to the natural man. The nations are fallen. They are not "born again." They have no claim on the "new creature." A Christian is free from their jurisdiction in all matters of conscience. He is not a citizen here. Morally he is a citizen of heaven at the mercy of this world, to be persecuted, except as God protects him. The nations are in rebellion against God. He cannot fight, for or against any one. How few have a clear vision of this matter. He may not even strive for his legitimate rights.

Christians cannot contemplate killing. It is utterly foreign to the spirit of their calling. A real Christian cannot take part in war. He has no part in the matter of judgment, but rather mercy. Unregenerate government will naturally misunderstand him. But they have absolutely nothing to fear from him. We are forbidden in time of war to aid (do good to) the enemy. But the Gospel commands us to "do good unto all men" (Gal 6:10). What then shall we do? Of course we are not to aid the enemy to harm others. That would be neither neutral or Christian. "But I say unto you that ye resist not evil" (Matt 5:39). We may not seek to injure an enemy, even in

"Christian Citizenship"

self-defense, for that will not tend to the winning of him to Christ. It was Christ's suffering love, in non-resistance, that won us to Him.

Sanctity only surrounds government edict so long as its mandates are in keeping with the Word of God. Could the early Christians have obeyed the mandates of the Roman government when they involved the abuse of their conscience in disobedience to the Gospel? Certainly not! Government mandate must be obeyed by the Christian so far as it ministers "for good," for righteous living, etc. But God never calls a Christian as an avenger, nor to protect himself or others by violence against men. His whole calling is very different. War in its very nature, be it offensive or defensive, violates the word of God for Christians. It can in no sense be accommodated to the teachings and spirit of the Gospel.

God's commands to His children are above even the decrees of fallen governments. Are there any governments in the world today obeying God, or at all Christian? Then what is a Christian's duty but to obey God, though he may even have to disobey government edict? War has no authority to change the code of morals for the Christian. What is wrong for a Christian in time of peace is equally wrong in time of war. He has no more right to attack a State enemy in time of war than he has to attack a private, personal foe. He is certainly not justified in sinning because of government decree. If government were to command the Christians to deny God, as Antichrist will do, what should they do? They are doing that in Russia now.

When the heathen became converted in the first centuries they were outlawed by government and their property confiscated. They "took joyfully the spoiling of their goods." The Jews and Romans could not destroy Jesus' arguments, so they destroyed Him. If the kingdom of this world were Christ's, John would have written,—"The kingdoms of this world are become the Kingdom's of our Lord, and of His Christ" (Rev 11:15). John wrote prophetically of a future time in the end.

The traditional sanctity thrown about Government mandate (right or wrong), has become one of the most subtle and powerful dangers for the Christian. It involves real sacrifice to withstand this false idea.

"Lifting up holy hands, without wrath or doubting" (1 Tim 2:8). Can a Christian do this and go to war? No! The Christian owes no duty to the call to war. It is a call in the wrong direction for him, away from God. "From whence come wars and fightings? Come they not hence, even of your lusts?" (Jas 4:1) We are to obey the legitimate laws of the land, for "conscience sake." There is no hint here that a Christian should ever go to war. In the very same connection we are commanded distinctly, "Thou shalt not kill" (Rom 13:9). A government agent said to some objecting brethren, "To hell with your conscience!"

One of the greatest crimes of the late war was that of robbing the church of her sacred calling and "pilgrim" role, turning her aside from the saving of souls, to plunge into the vortex of world politics and patriotism, with all its fallen prejudices and preferences, avarices, cruelties, hates and murders. The church has fallen before the god of War, in the place of Dagon falling before the Ark of God. What does the church look like on the human field of battle, all stained with human gore?

Are we already arrived at a place where we cannot tell God from devil? A man who has not the courage to be the only Christian in the world if need be, and remain true to God, is not yet much of a Christian. We have got to stand the test individually, not as a body. Small wonder Christians are so hazy on the war question, when they can hate their fellow Christians, ready to do them harm by voice and pen, if not by actual physical violence.

In place of responding joyfully to the call to suffer for Christ, most Christians are busy looking for a way to avoid such sufferings. They adore the history of the early martyrs who suffered, but condemn all present day martyrdom for Christ. The early disciples departed from the presence of the council, "rejoicing that they were counted worthy to suffer shame for His name" (Acts 5:41). A beautiful bunch of hypocrites most of us are! We praise up dead saints eloquently and curse down living ones fervently.

May God's command to Christians be set aside by government edict? The early Christians found themselves squarely up against the earthly governments of their day. They were practically outlawed by them. We imagine the Antichrist will seek to set aside all the commands of God, by government decree. Nations do not worship the gods of Rome today, but they worship gods of gold, price, avarice, etc., etc.

Traditional sanctity has been thrown around government edict, right or wrong, until most people are inclined to accept the situation as Gospel, or at least in place of the Gospel. It is another traditional god to be delivered from. Daniel was ordered by government edict, by law of Medes and Persians that could not be altered, not to pray to his God. Did he obey? Certainly not! And did God honor him in his stand? Most assuredly! We ought always to obey God rather than men.

The governments of this world have always persecuted the real Christians, while worshipping false gods, either those of Rome, or the modern ones of national jealousy, territorial greed, etc., etc. The governments of earth began by persecuting the Christians. They will end their career at the same God-defying business. We had mob law during the war.

If it were the duty of Christians to go to war in obedience to the rulers, then it would be their duty on one side as much as on another. Government would be an arbitrary god, without reason. Who is government, but the people?

Possibly the war might have stopped short of its worst stages had the Allies been willing to forego their prospect of complete commercial supremacy, and cherished revenge on the Kaiser, who plead with Wilson to stop the war. "Peace without victory." We all remember the cry. Jesus prayed, "Father, forgive them!"

Shall Christians fight under government compulsion? Must God be disobeyed to obey government decree? The traditional god of government edict in the time of war precedes the authority of God Almighty with most Christians. It is Christ or Caesar. That is the issue.

The Church is no place to flaunt flags of national preference. God's grace and Gospel are international. Christ died for all men. Antichrist means to run the church by government edict. Then we will have State and Church. The State will dictate to the Church. The flags represent fallen nations, with fallen nationalistic, sectional prides, ambitions, etc., that breed strife, enmity, jealousy and war, for they are without Christ. We do not belong to them.[1]

---

1. Bartleman, *Christian Citizenship*, 1–2.

31

War and the Christian

Frank Bartleman

After 1921

"When they are saying, 'Peace and safety,' then sudden destruction cometh upon them" (1 Thess 5:3). This is our excuse for reviving this subject at this time. The worst wars are undoubtedly yet to come.

Let it be understood that the following message is to Christians: "For what have I to do to judge them that are without? Do not ye judge them that are within, but them that are without God judgeth?" (1 Cor 5:12).

To show the popular attitude that exists on the matter of war, we quote the following excerpts from a variety of sources:

The Rev Reginald Campbell, the most popular preacher in England, was one of the first to assert that the British soldier who gave his life in this war was sure of heaven. This expression was widely quoted by British chaplains and recruiting officers, and helped to stimulate patriotic feeling."—Los Angeles Examiner, Oct. 27, 1918.

An Australian writer reports, May, 1916: "The Governor of this State said last year at a meeting of the Bible Society (Western Australia,) "Soldiers fighting and dying in this conflict, go straight to heaven, whatever their previous lives may have been."

Dr. Gordon, leading clergyman of Canada, said in substance: "The uniform of King George upon a soldier boy is a sure passport to heaven, and God, Himself, cannot keep a young man out of heaven who dies with the British uniform upon him."

A writer in Canada says: "A soldier said to a Christian the other day, "They tell us if we die in battle we shall be sure to go to heaven." The sacrifice of these human lives is set forth as being sufficient to merit heaven without the atoning work of Christ. A preacher tells his audience that to die in such a war as this is "a passport to heaven," and that death in such a cause is "a modern re-enacting of the sacrifice of Christ, Himself."

The Mohammedan leaders have said to their soldiers, "The gates of Paradise are under the shade of swords; he who dies fighting for the faith will assuredly gain admission there." And men today in Christian England, would send you forth to fight, telling you that your death will be an expiation for all your sins. (The same thing.)

A brother wrote from Canada during the war: "Wives and mothers and all women are called upon to hiss (snakes hiss) at every man who is eligible to recruit. Further they are making a house-to-house canvass to learn who means to fight. Churches are used for recruiting services. The Antichrist is getting possession of the House of God, and is setting up his image in the hearts of the people. Pray for the brethren in patriotic, devil-crazed Canada."

A certain writer said, during the war: "As the kings have sent their subjects to war, the clergy have stood by the kings and said, in substance, "Push on your war of destruction; God is with you, and we will pray His blessing upon your army." Which army?

The clergy have urged the young men to enter this war. Notwithstanding the fact that the Lord has taught that no murderer shall enter His Kingdom, the clergy teach that he who dies while engaged in war upon the battlefield has an abundant entrance into heaven.

Dr. Krehbiel, authority on International Relations, of Stanford University, said: "The national system strikes a terrific blow at religion. Every nation asserts God to be on its side. That is virtually extending conscription to God."

Dr. Peter Ainslie, Pastor of the Christian Temple, Baltimore, said: "More than to any other source the cause of the great war lies at the door of the Church."

Rabbi Wise of New York City said, during the war: "The failure of the churches and synagogues to maintain leadership over the people was the cause of the present war. They have enthroned a war devil in place of God."

Rev Scott Anderson said of the military during the war: "As a class in upholding war, bloody war, in trying to drag the God of Love, the friend of all men and the Prince of Peace into this great tragedy, they (the ministry) are blaspheming that worthy name more than all others combined."

"K.C.B.," whose column appeared daily in the Los Angeles Examiner, wrote as follows: "They are floating flags of challenge over the houses that were built for Him who knows no flag nor boundary. From what I learned of the Lord when I went to church I'm sure He doesn't want any flag on His churches over here, or in Germany, or anywhere else."

Another writer says: "Has there ever been a more terrible bankruptcy of a whole creed than that of historical Christianity in the face of this war?"

The Editor of the Los Angeles Examiner wrote, November, 1921: "All the traditions and influences and precepts of humanity and religion were cast aside by common consent. The ministers of the mild and gentle Jesus and the men of art and literature and learning and scientific pursuits, vied with the most brutal and ignorant and hateful elements of the baser sort, in screaming for more slaughter, more blood, more human agony."

Another writer says: "It seems that the demon forces of hell have been turned loose upon the world. The great majority of the criminals are young men. What wonder when just a short time ago the nations of the world were arrayed against each other in mortal combat. The youth of the world were taught the game of war. He who could inflict the greatest punishment and suffering on the enemy was counted the greatest hero. To rob the enemy of his wealth and property, and to destroy his life is a part of the game of war. The youth have been schooled in this for years. Many learned to love it, with no regard for the life of others, and little for their own.

Today these same young men are turned loose upon society. Some are out of employment and money. Many do not want work. Life seems humdrum and monotonous. They crave excitement and blood-curdling experiences. The result is the hold-ups, robberies, murders and crimes of every description. Because we have sowed the wind we are reaping the whirlwind."

Edward H. White, State Parole Officer of California, says: "Crime is increasing at an alarming rate. San Quentin Penitentiary now holds more than 100 over its capacity. 60 per cent of the prisoners are under 30 years of age. 40 per cent are under 25. The old prisoner is hardly known in San Quentin now. Most crime is committed by young fellows, most of whom are returned from war. Some earned as high as $15 or $20 a day, at good positions."

A writer says, concerning the use of Chinese (and Africans, etc.) during the war: "The Chinese laborers will go back to China thoroughly equipped to teach China's 400,000,000 how to make ammunition with which to destroy the white race, when the time comes for Asia to do that. One of the worst results of this European War is the instruction of the yellow races in the art of destroying human beings by the wholesale—a lesson which they will not be slow to repeat upon the heads of the Caucasian race. They are sowing the wind which will yet become the whirlwind to destroy their own peoples and their own civilizations. There never was such an exhibition of suicidal madness on such a huge scale." Someone said in the beginning of the war that "the civilized, Christian nations are committing hari-kari (suicide) on the back door steps of Japan."

Gen. Sherman said: "War is hell."

The Duke of Wellington said: "War is a detestable thing. If you had seen but one day of war, you would pray God that you might never see another."

Geo. Fox, leader of the Quakers, said: "I cannot fight, for the spirit of war is slain within me."

Sydney Smith said: "God is forgotten in war; every principle of Christianity is trampled upon."

Tertullian said: "Our religion teaches us that it is better to be killed than to kill."

Russell Lowell said: "If you take a sword and draw it, and go stick a fellow through, government won't have to answer for it, God will send the bill to you."

"The refusal of the Christians to bear arms lasted for the first two or three centuries. It was usual for a solder to lay down his sword when he accepted the truth of Christ. The declaration of their faith has become historic: "I am a Christian, and therefore I cannot fight."

A testimony was written by a Holiness professor in the trenches of France. He said he was sanctified with a gun across his knees, ready to go "over the top" at any moment. This testimony was O.K'd. by the office force of a Holiness paper.

One of the leading Statesmen of France declared in the Senate, since the war began, that they had blotted out the light of the Heavens, and blasphemously said that they had ended God's interference with the affairs of France. His blasphemy was received with enthusiasm and the Senate ordered that part of his speech to be placarded in every town and village in France.

Mr. Asquith, Prime Minister of England, declared that "conscientious objectors" would be treated with the "utmost rigor," while his successor, Lloyd George, said in the House of Commons that he would "only consider the best means of making the path of 'conscientious objectors' a very hard one."

One of the declarations of the American Legion is: "We shall use our influence to prolong the prison sentences of conscientious objectors to war and to have army officers punished for showing leniency toward them."

News comes from Russia that practically all the Evangelical believers are refusing to take up arms in the civil war, either for or against the Bolsheviks, saying that the arms of their warfare must be spiritual and not carnal.

From Germany comes most interesting news. Many of the German Christians refused to bear arms, and were shot in consequence. At a recent meeting in Berlin, Pastor Paul, his face haggard and thin through the great privations of the last five years, stood up and said: "By the grace of God, we, as a Pentecostal people, will never lift up the sword again for any cause." And with one voice the large company of Pentecostal people present proclaimed that to be their firm purpose and determination.

Very recently Fort Leavenworth (our National Prison) contained at one time 500 to 800 Christian prisoners. Some of them died in the prison because of the cruelties inflicted upon them. Others were sent home a physical wreck. Terrible cruelties were perpetrated on Christian objectors at Alcatraz. They were beaten, starved, frozen, stretched up by the hands, etc., until much of the treatment by their "tormentors" reads like the "Inquisition." Many died from the results of this treatment, and for no other crime than that they were real "Christians."

A brother writes from Scotland of conditions in Britain during the war: "Godly men of all ages were arrested and thrown into prison—Evangelists, Teachers and Preachers, City Missionaries and Christian Workers of practically all denominations, men whose moral and spiritual value were worth more to the nation than a dozen armies. Those first to be arrested were most brutally treated—being struck and kicked and subjected to many indignities—until the long list of crimes appalled many, and serious protest in Parliament and out of it, served to somewhat lessen the rigor of these barbaric cruelties.

What the future will bring we know. We anticipate further persecution—for the nearer we approach the end of the age, the more bitter will become Satan's wrath, as he perceives his time shortening and his certain doom approaching.

"Pilgrims" toward a "better land" were forced into training camps, beaten with clubs, prodded with bayonets, choked and kicked mercilessly.

In England the prisons were emptied of their criminal population—thieves, embezzlers and scoundrels of every type, and these were sent into the army (hardened to commit any crime,) while the saints of God were thrust into their cells and subjected to every possible hurt and indignity. In British prisons are lying some of God's choicest saints because of their loyalty to Christ.

Hundreds of true and faithful men of God have been incarcerated for the Word of God and the Testimony of Jesus Christ. Some have lost their lives through disease brought on by the rigors of the persecution. A few of these young men were so brutally beaten again and again that mind and body were completely exhausted."[1]

A British writer says: "Not for centuries has the professing church's failure called so loudly for the Divine judgment on her as at this juncture."

Again the writer from Scotland says: "None were more astonished as the warlike attitude of leading Christians and the eagerness of so many of them to rush out and kill than were the War Office authorities themselves. (What a terrible indictment!)"

The attitude of the churches has been contrary to Christ and Christianity. Soon the whole professing church will suffer the judgment of God—for judgment must first begin at the House of God (1 Peter 4:17). (It has begun.)

Some of the well-known Evangelists have become little better than recruiting sergeants, and scores of young men were sent to fight directly through them.

The whole professing church has apostatized from Christ, marking her apostasy by her eager vindication of the saints' participation in war. The act of the so-called churches and ministers flinging themselves into war only exposes the hollowness of their pretensions.

What an opportunity the believers of every nation had when this war began! (To refuse to fight because they were Christians. That would have stopped the war. The leaders in the war themselves were professed Christians.) And what an opportunity lost! (Lost forever.)

Outside the church, judgment belongs to God alone, and if He uses one nation to chastise another for its sins, woe be to the saint who is foolhardy enough to join the conflict.

Many Christian young men have been slain in battle, particularly the sons of leading teachers, ministers and evangelists, who have with blood guiltiness, incited the saints to take up the weapons of carnal warfare.

---

1. There is no beginning quotation mark in the original.

The Chairman at a large meeting of Christians remarked publicly on the presence of so many young men, and wished there had been a recruiting sergeant there. (They would be glad now to see a few young men in Christian meetings, since the war.)

In most Christian Assemblies the "war spirit" has been so predominant during the last few years that one dared not pray publicly for God's saints in prison without being assailed by a torrent of abuse. One leading brother said publicly in a meeting that if he had his way "they would every one (the conscientious objectors) be shot."—So writes our correspondent from Scotland.

It was the custom in a certain, central Pentecostal Mission in London during the war to open each meeting with what the leader was pleased to call "their War Hymn." The author himself heard them sing it, in the early part of the war. We give some sample lines: "When the trumpet call, resounding, speeds them forward to the fight. For the shock and strain of conflict, gird them with Thy constant might. Homeward bring our valiant kinsmen, crowned with lasting victory. Be their Captain, Guide and Savior, till the world's lust war is o'er," etc. What has a Christian to do with that?

And now we hear of another proposed "Holy War," in Poland. A mass meeting has been recently held in Poland attended by 3000 people, by the Anti-Semitic League. The meeting called the Polish people to a "holy war of Christians against the Jews." We are fed up on "holy wars." Since the devil got sanctified (?) we have had nothing but holy wars. And hell has been turned loose. We wonder what the "Reds" think of this latest move in Poland to "convert" them? They say most of the Bolsheviki are Jews. No doubt this will impress them still further with the beauty and desirability of Christianity (so-called). The Greek Church has given them a taste of it for some hundreds of years in Russia. Seriously, is it any wonder the Jews are not converted?

Let us take a glance at prospective modern warfare, subject to much greater efficiency, no doubt, with time.

"Washington exhibits a tiny bottle filled with killing gas so deadly that the German gas would be infants' food compared with it. Dropped by fliers in quantities this poison would have killed the millions in Berlin or any great city. This country was making the gas at the rate of ten tons a day when war ended.—(Arthur Brisbane.)

In England flame throwers have been invented capable of licking up everything in their path, and these will be brought to a high degree of perfection. A man has perfected an apparatus by means of which ultra-red rays can be applied to blow up distant battleships and fortresses. America has already successfully operated a great battleship with electricity, guiding, fueling, and discharging the guns at will, without the presence of a single man on board.

One writer says: "Attacking nations in the future will make no foolish warning declarations of war. They will strike first, and the striking will be terrible beyond description, with gases, invisible rays, and even with germs. The great cities will be totally destroyed, the great mass of men, women and children will be dead, even the land will be useless, and the stench of a great festering will make disgusting the earth. After the recent war, the world goes about on crutches, staring with bleary eyes. After the next it will have no limbs at all, and it will be cursing blind." (Not a bit exaggerated. Who wants to see more war?)

A precious mother, whose son died in one of our penitentiaries from extreme exposure in a damp cell and lack of care when sick, writes that she suffered equally with her boys in insults, scorn and slurring remarks heaped upon her, even by many Pentecostal professors. Her boy was a precious, consistent saint of God. All that he was guilty of was of being too true to Jesus to go and kill his fellow creatures, against whom he felt no ill and who had never done him any harm. The Chaplain of the prison where he died was a Roman Catholic and the Commandant a Nazarene. And so this precious young life was lost to the world and possibly to the mission field, and all in the name of the murderous, horrible Moloch of war. "Thou shalt not give any of thy seed to make them pass through the fire to Molech."—Lev. 18:21.

We have nothing good to say of the purpose of the German war-lords in going to war. Doubtless they were as guilty of any. But we confess we first began to get our eyes open when we passed through London, en route for home. There every business house was placarded in large letters. "Death to German trade," "Our war on German trade." Delivery wagons were forced to carry these banners, or their owners be forced to carry these banners, or their owners be forced out of business. It looked like purely a commercial war. When England placarded all the principal cities with huge mottoes, "Trust in Kitchener," God let him sink. They no longer trusted in God.

Our first introduction to "church patriotism" was in England, in 1910. There we found all the old musty war banners, that had been taken from other nations in battle for centuries, stacked up in God's house of worship.

Busts of all the leading Generals, who had led the most men to death, and sent the most men to hell, occupied the prominent niches in the Chapels. Honored as paragon saints. This custom prevails in Christian (?) nations pretty much all over Europe. We have now adopted it in America.

It is not right to curse our enemies simply because it is popular. During the war there was little else left for a preacher to do, especially if he wanted to be popular. The Gospel was scarcely allowed to be preached. One could not preach "love your enemies," or even "pray for them" honestly. To do so brought down a storm upon our heads. To be a Christian meant to be denominated "pro-German." Spies haunted every little Pentecostal meeting. It was almost as difficult to preach the Gospel as in Russia before the war. One did not know what they dared preach. The popular "war-slogan" was "Watch your neighbor," until very few people had any neighbors. They were all enemies. The rules made a "scape-goat" of the Kaiser by common consent. They were suddenly transformed into angels. They laid all their sins upon him.

"Onward Christian soldiers, marching as to war," was sung as a patriotic hymn in most of the churches, while Christians (?) rushed to battle to murder one another. The leaders in the war were professed Christians, heads of their churches, "rulers by divine right," etc., etc. Worse than Crusader and Moslem, Cross and Crescent. They had to borrow the money of the poor Jew and call on the Heathen to help them out. They will have to pay it back all right. The "poor Jew" will soon be on top.

The "Crusaders" tried to convert the Moslem Turk with the sword. He was pretty good at that game himself. The Greek Church in Russia has waged war against the Jew for centuries. The "massacres" and "pogroms" are world-known. The Reds (largely Jews) are objecting. Can we expect the Jew to accept the Christ of the system under which he has for so long time suffered so atrociously and unjustly? About all the Socialists known of Christ in Europe is what they have suffered at the hands of the Autocratic, capitalistic classes, who have claimed to be sole custodians of the Gospel.

Any system must be radically wrong that forbids, or even discourages, the preaching of the Gospel. Has the Gospel changed? Gospel before the war was surely Gospel during the war. But we did not hear much of it. Most people were preaching "patriotism." The churches were recruiting stations. (They had been political platforms, largely.)

Is war the work of the church—Christ's commission? Men who preached so clearly and nobly before the war, against war, all seemed suddenly to get the lock-jaw. It was about to cost them something. They became "dumb dogs" (D.D.'s.) They could not bark. There were few applicants for martyrs' crowns. Yet what a noble opportunity to "Dare to be a Daniel, dare to stand alone. Dare to have a purpose firm, and dare to make it known." All got busy "saving their lives." They have failed their Lord, like Peter, in the crisis. "They all forsook Him, and fled." The Church lost her opportunity during the war. She cannot escape the penalty for the same.

The Church's sole business is to evangelize the world, and that as quickly as possible. The churches have been shot full of holes through participation in the war. They must repent, be cleansed from blood, if they can ever expect to have a Revival. In England during the war it was suggested that the nation observe a day of humiliation and prayer. The so-called Spiritual leaders were loudest in disclaiming any need of humiliation, while the authorities removed the offending word.

War is contrary to the whole Spirit and teaching of Christ. Any one going into war is bound to lose out. Christ's kingdom is "not of this world." If so, "then would His servants fight." When first saved you could not have been induced to harm your own worst enemy. What then has happened? The church has lost her "first love." War is "licensed" murder.

When heathen solders became converted they threw down their arms. Jesus instructed the soldiers to "do violence to no man." He could not call them out of the army. He was not fighting governments. His "time was not yet come." Dispensationally the "new birth" had not yet arrived.

No Christian going into war can ever be quite the same again. He has lost the opportunity, possibly of a life-time, of standing true to Christ in a supreme test. For here is the supreme test of a Christian, to be killed rather than to kill. He can never forget his participation in the war, and his betrayal of the principles of the Christ who died for all men. A Christian must refuse to obey any spirit contrary to the teachings of the Scripture. Hate, murder, lust, etc., none of them fruits of the Spirit. No one can kill a man, and yet love him. We have got to love all men alike. War cannot be Christian. Ask the boys in camp, or on the battlefield. They will tell you it is hell, from end to end. Compare it with the Sermon on the Mount.

We have two reasons for reviving the war question at this time. A past and a future one. First, repentance must be forthcoming on the part of the Christian. Second, "If thou hast run with the footmen and they have wearied thee, then how canst thou content with horses?" (Rev 6) or, "how wilt thou do in the swelling of Jordan?" (Jer 12:5).

The Christian is first a witness, then a "martyr." He is never a judge or avenger. The Pentecostal people failed to stand by the Lord. What can we expect of the churches? Where will God get His martyrs for these "last days?" Abject fear reigns in the hearts of most believers. They fear the edicts of men more than God. Most would even fear to "visit a brother in prison" for conscience sake. Paul prayed, The Lord grant mercy unto the house of Onesiphorus; for he was not ashamed of my chain." Paul was also a prisoner, for the Gospel's sake.

Let us look at some of the methods of war. The Japs (usually freely cursed,) were held up as saints and liberators of the human race, during the war. Yet Japan is practically an absolute monarchy. Even tender children were persecuted, unbearably if they did not put their pennies into war stamps. They were forced, under pain of punishment both for themselves and parents, to take part in the war. They were subjected to forced lectures calculated to instill hatred and murder in their little lives for the enemy. Lying propaganda was freely used. In fact an office was created for that purpose. The people went mad. Teachers even threatened to withhold grade promotions from children who were opposed to working for the war. It was a trying time for Christian parents. One can never forget it fully.

War is insanity, madness. A great insane asylum turned out of doors. Language was allowed during the war, and sin winked at, that will curse the next generation. Magazines were filled with war literature, all intended to inspire hate in the readers. A supreme effort was made to harden the nation for war. And it succeeded. There is very little response now to the Gospel. The soldiers especially were ruined, morally and physically. Of course they ought to know where to stop. But they do not. When you train the youth of the nation for fighting machines, and send them forth to kill, they cannot be remodeled with a mere magician's wave of the hand. It takes much longer to make saints than devils.

War belongs to the old creation, to the "first Adam," the fallen nature. It is unregenerate and under the "curse" fully. "In the beginning it was not so." It is not the Christian's calling. We are "new creatures," in the "second Adam," regenerated, citizens of a heavenly country. "Old things are passed away, behold, all things are become new." Our "citizenship is in heaven." We have no more business with the politics of this world than a Foreign Ambassador has meddling with the politics of the country to which he is sent. He is to represent his country. We are "ambassadors for Christ" at a foreign court. Let us represent our country faithfully. If Jesus had shown any other spirit than love on the cross, the atonement would have been marred and rendered worthless. We are of the same Spirit.

The Christian in war-time is up against the real thing. He is practically asked to deny Christ. It is "Good-bye God until the end of the war." There can be no greater test of one's faithfulness. The way real Christians were persecuted during the war ought to be sufficient to determine for any thinking man where wars come from. In times of war one discovers in reality who is the "prince of this world." Then must he decide where his citizenship really is. The devil will soon discover also where the real Christian stands. They will soon be brought face to face. Most Christians know the right in such a case. But they will not suffer the consequences for Christ.

Can a Christian be a citizen of this world, when at the will of a handful of exploiters the lives and property of the common people can be commandeered without a protest? Patriotism in most cases has been proven to spell "Graft." "Dollar" patriotism. War bonds are reduced in price until the poor man is either forced or frightened into unloading. Then they suddenly soar above par. Stung again! They are now in the hands of the very patriotic Broker. The innocent are sent to do the killing, and be killed. Those responsible for the wars are generally beyond its reach.

The poor must live on half rations. The sick must die. "A survival of the fittest." That is the way to produce a strong nation. The newspaper of today is not fit to enter a Christian home, with children. We cannot buy new clothes. We cannot buy good food. We cannot travel. Rent prices are criminally high. They tell us nothing can be done. But, why? They can commandeer a nation, when they want to.

The persecution of Christians during the war was in many cases equal to that of the first century. Many who refused to fight were literally "martyred," in a Christian (?) land. The regular course was to deliver them first to an Army bully, who would give them the "third degree," that is, beat them up unmercifully, to make them fight back. After that they were delivered over to the "tormentors," in the penitentiaries, etc. God will judge the guilty ones in this business. One's heart burns to think of these Christian "martyrs," who in many cases literally laid down their lives rather than partake of the damning virus of war, fail Christ and lose their souls.

A "war church" is a Harlot church. It persecutes the true children of God. Slave of tradition and cowardly fear, she traitorously hands over the true children of God to a demonized state to destroy them. As the Jewish High Church handed Jesus over to the Romans, for destruction. The church persecuted its "pacifists" members with the bitterness of hell itself during the war. She had to walk in the light, or persecute those who did. The old patriotic Harlot, ridden by the Beast. Religion and State unite against the Christ. She would deliver us over today, if possible, for telling her the truth. But we must, like John the Baptist, be faithful to Church and State.

War is demoralizing. It is a disastrous in the end to victor as to vanquished. Napoleon conquered by force. Jesus conquered by love (not hate.) But some may say, "If we are attacked by a heathen nation? What then?" We answer, would the missionary kill a heathen, if attacked by him? My message is to Christians. If the church had obeyed her commission from God, to spend all her energies in the power of the Holy Ghost, in preaching the Gospel to the heathen there would be no such situation. But, if there were the Christian would have no more right to take life, to kill his enemy.

The spirit of the Antichrist is causing the saints to fear. It is binding their conscience, for the rule of Antichrist. The war has paved the way definitely for this issue. The "mark of the Beast" comes gradually. It will soon mean bondage, or "Siberia." The apostate church will not repent of her sin in going into war. She will go on with her hypocritical pretensions, and carnal efforts at world betterment.

Judgment has already "begun at the house of God." We see its beginnings in Europe. They shall "burn her utterly with fire. For God hath put it in their hearts to fulfill His will" (Rev 17:16, 17). The terrible Reds are doing this to the false church systems today. The churches have failed God. He is "spuing" them out. The war spirit has utterly ruined them. The "time of their ignorance" God may have "winked at" ("passed over").

The State system (Church and State) will no doubt develop in America, in order to bring her in the same condition as the European nations. Then revolt will come. The misrule of the Caesars will increase. Rulers are supposed to be a "terror to the evil," not to God's children. And they are God's ministers "for good," not for evil. The usurpation of power by the "man of sin" is on the increase, to culminate in the rule of the Antichrist. Antichrist will be a combination of Religion and Rule. He will head all government.

A flood of "lawlessness" is let loose upon the nations. They have rejected God. They have run their course. Their times are about full. The Lord seems to have no further particular purpose for them in His will. That is evidently why the Statesmen are confused. The war has left everything in a whirl. And the saints who have lost their "pilgrim" role are also in a whirl. God has rejected the nations. Antichrist is soon destined to appear.

Lawlessness hastens to the end. The world has lost its bearings. The nations will be broken to pieces, removed to pave the way for the universal reign of the terrible Antichrist, the "Lawless One." Such is the teaching of the Word of God. The only hope for anyone is to seek God. "Be patient, brethren, unto the coming of the Lord" (Jas 5:7). "Look up, and life up your heads, for your redemption draweth nigh" (Luke 21:28).[2]

---

2. Bartleman, *War and the Christian*.

32

"From the Pentecostal Viewpoint"
Stanley Frodsham
1924

A Long Time Dead

BILLY BRAY WAS ONCE asked, "How are things getting on in the world?" Billy answered, "I have been such long time dead that I don't know." His passion for evangelism gave him no time for the study of current events. Less newspaper and more Bible will be as good for us as it was for this earnest evangelists.

Heart Preparations

There are, however, some things happening in the world today that we believe all of God's saints should know in order that they might pray intelligently and that they may be prepared for the coming events that are already casting their ugly shadows before. The best preparation for things to come is a good grounding in the principles of the Word of God. "Man shall not live by bread alone but by every word that proceedeth out of the mouth of God." The man who knows the Word knows the will of God, and knows how to act under every circumstance that may arise.

Darkening Clouds

Our attention has been called to an article that appeared in the Dearborn Independent of April 12. The writer, Samuel Crowther, has been spending some months in Europe to report on the war conditions. Before he went, he thought that another was impossible, that the people were tired of war, that there was no more money for war, that everyone was sick of it. But after visiting nearly every country in Europe, talking with politicians, industrialists, labor leaders, and the man in the street, he states the question is not, "Will there be another war" but "When and where will the next war be?"

Conditions Today

After telling of the grievances he found in almost every country, grievances that have been a direct result of the Versailles treaty, for each county which received territory thought it got less than its due, and each country which lost territory claims it lost an integral part of its population,"[1] this writer states, (1) There are today more men under arms in Europe than in 1914, and at least eight countries are on a war footing. (2) There are more active causes for war, and these causes are being more actively agitated than at any time within the past fifty years. (3) Except in England, the dread of war does not exist. The people think war preferable to the way they are now living—for somehow soldiers get enough to eat. He further states, "These people in Europe are thinking of war largely because they have precious little else to think about. They are hungry, they are desperate, and they are armed. The big war did not teach them the futility of war. They mostly think that the war stopped too soon and that they were juggled out of their rights by peace. This applies equally to the victors and the vanquished." He believes that another war is inevitable.

A General's Viewpoint

A new book has recently been written by Brigadier General Morgan, the InterAllied Commissioner of Control. He says in this book:

> Germany found herself by the treaty of Versailles a captive giant in the hands of Europe, her looks shorn, her eyes put out—an object of derision to some, of contempt to others, of antipathy to all. Her captors put her to grind for them and girt her roundabout with a wall of steel, saying, "Our God hath delivered our enemy into our hands." Now in the temple of European society there are two pillars upon which the whole of that temple rests—one is the pillar of credit, the other is the pillar of law, the law is only another name

---

1. The first quotation mark is missing from original.

for moral order. And I sometimes think that like the captive giant in the Temple of Gaza, Germany, in her agony and her shame, is putting forth her hands to grasp the two pillars upon which European civilization rests and has breathed a prayer, "O Lord God, remember me, I pray Thee and strengthen me. I pray Thee, only this once. O God, that I may be avenged upon mine enemies." If she is to go down into the abyss, she is determined to drag all Europe down with her; and I think that such a catastrophic policy is still within her power.

A General's Warning

He further says, "What a field you have left for exploitation by some great military adventurer of German blood, who, calling in the dark forces of Russia, will appeal to sixty millions of German people so desperate that they have nothing left to lose, and sweep like an avalanche across the West." He later adds, "The peace of the world is not to be assured by a peace recommendation from The Hague or a peace circular from Geneva, nor will any international reduction or standardization of military establishments achieve it. Nothing but what the old Puritans called 'a change of heart' in the sons of men can ensue it."

The Friends' Stand

What will be the attitude of God's children should war come? The Quakers have come out boldly at their Philadelphia meeting this year. They passed the following minute and their Peace and Service Committee was instructed to send the same to the officials of the various churches and to the religious press. The minute reads as follows: "This meeting desires to reaffirm its belief that the primary loyalty of all Christians is due God, our Father, and all His human family. We believe that the whole system of determining right by violence and destruction rather than by friendly conference and negotiation is fundamentally wrong, inefficient and unchristian. We call upon Christian people of whatever sect or creed to join in renouncing for the future all participation in war, and to seek through our national representatives such international organizational as will supply peaceful methods of dealing with all international differences. We also urge upon Christians consideration of inter-class an interracial problems and an effort to solve them through good will and understanding." When the editor of the paper received a copy and handed the same to the Chairman of the Council, Brother Welch expressed the warmest sympathy for the sentiments of the Friends. The statement on our Council minutes concerning non–participation in war is somewhat stronger than the above.

An Indictment

About three years ago, 100,000 ministers of this country on a given Sunday appealed for disarmament. In August 1923, Christian leaders from twenty-five nations met at Copenhagan and agreed that, "To the mind of Christ war is an abomination, and His followers should, step by step, take action to make it impossible." A writer in the Nation protested, "What is wanted is a Christian statesman who will say, 'This war is against the will of God at the moment when this war is in preparation, or in action.' What is the use of a 'message' which is always delivered when it is not immediately relevant. The time for our church leaders to declare for peace is when a war is on. In the hour of man's greatest agony the Christian churches in every land brought no gift of healing, but held the clothes of those who stoned humanity."

Christ's Instructions

The Master gave the last word on this subject: "Ye have heard that it hath been said, Thou shalt love thy neighbor, and hate thine enemy. But I say unto you, Love your enemies, bless them that curse you, do good to them that hate you, and pray for them which despitefully use you, and persecute you; that ye may be children of your Father which is in heaven: for He maketh his sun to rise on the evil and on the good, and sendeth rain upon the just and on the unjust." He further stated, "They that take the sword shall perish by the sword." The Father gave witness to the gracious words that proceeded from the mouth of the Lord Jesus with a very definite command, "This is my beloved Son, hear ye him." We reject absolutely that false teaching that the words of Christ are "law and not grace," and that the Sermon on the Mount is "neither the privilege nor the duty of the church."

The Early Church

What was the attitude of the early church towards war? "In the first two centuries of our era, so swordless was the church of Christ, that Celsus, the Gnostic, in the first written attack ever made on the Christian faith, grounds his censure on this very fact, and says, "The State receives no help in war from the Christians; and if all men were to follow the example, the Sovereign would be deserted and the world would fall into the hands of barbarians." Origen gave this profound answer: "The question is—What would happen if the Romans should be persuaded to adopt the principles of the Christian? This is my answer—We say that if two of us shall agree on earth as touching anything that they shall ask, it shall be done for them by the Father who is in heaven. What, then, are we to expect, if not only a very few should agree, as at present, but the whole empire of Rome? They would pray to the Word, who of old said to the Hebrews, when pursued by the Egyptians, "The Lord shall fight for you, and ye shall hold your peace." No mortal knows what could not be got, by man, or class, or nation, or world, by substituting prayer for war. "Ye have not, James says, 'because ye ask not.'"

The Cause of Wars

Commenting on Jas 4:1, Pastor D. M. Panton, from whom we have taken the above quotation, says, "'Whence come wars'—in both the New Testament and Septuagint, the word is always used of actual warfare—'and whence come fightings'—duels, brawls, bitter industrial conflicts—'among you?' Does war spring from defective politics, or secret diplomacy, or badly drawn frontiers, or mismanaged government? Whatever part these may play as a provocation, a far profounder cause is unmasked by the Holy Ghost: 'Come they not hence, even of your lusts' (pleasures: what pleases the lustful man)—'that war in your members?' The first battleground is the heart, which creates all consequent war: 'Ye lust, and have not: ye kill, and desire to have, and cannot obtain: ye fight and war.' Napoleon, with a flash of evil genius, once said to his brother Joseph: 'What a nation hates is—another nation.' Political pacifists lodge war in the wrong spot: they lodge it in human organization; God lodges it in human nature. Chemical dynamite is only the explosion of human dynamite; war is the everlasting battle between the 'haves' and 'have nots'; it is man's insatiable appetite for the earthly always baffled by the dead sea apples of the world: it is the devouring hunger of the human which only the Bread of God can appease."

The Only Remedy

At the close of the war, Field Marshall Earl Haig, the commander of the British forces, said, "The gospel of Christ is the world's only hope—the sole promise of world peace." What we need, as we quoted Brother R. A. Brown as saying recently, is a new revival, a revival that will sweep thousands into the kingdom and prepare them for the soon coming of Christ. The world will have its wars and its rumors of wars, but the child of God can have a peace that passeth all understanding, a peace that Christ left with us, a peace that He gives, a peace in which He expects us to live. When the love of God is shed abroad in our hearts by the Holy Ghost we cannot but love every man for whom Christ died. The psalmist said, "I am for peace: but when I speak, they are for war" (Ps 120:7). What will be the attitude of your heart when all the world is filled again with a lust for war?[2]

---

2. Frodsham, "From the Pentecostal Viewpoint," 4–5.

33

"War, the Bible, and the Christian" [Part 1]

Donald Gee

1930

TWELVE YEARS HAVE ROLLED by since the Armistice of November, 1918, virtually concluded the last Great War; and we are now able, in a calmer atmosphere, to reconsider carefully some of the burning issues of those hectic days.

Such a reconsideration is now opportune. Young people are growing up all around us who were mere children in 1914 to 1918. They had no personal share in the tremendous decisions which many were then compelled to make; yet should another such crisis arise (and it may not be so distant as we hope), they will be immediately compelled to make for themselves, as disciples of the Lord Jesus Christ, decisions of the very gravest importance. It is obviously foolish to wait until the storm breaks before preparation is made. Now, in a time of comparative calm, is the golden opportunity for prayerful study of the will of God revealed in His Word, and for earnest consecration to do that will at whatever cost, based upon solid conviction.

The Popular Attitude

It is almost universally conceded today that war is essentially evil, and a general desire to see it abolished is evidenced by the succession of leagues, pacts, conferences, etc., all aiming at making war more and more unlikely, and ultimately unthinkable. So deeply is this desire and attitude towards war imbedded in the popular mind that one of the slogans with which weary nations spurred themselves on in the last sickening conflict was the

"War, the Bible, and the Christian" [Part 1]

hope that it was the "war to end war." It is a striking commentary upon the truth of the now almost rejected doctrine of inbred sin in the human race, that, while the nations loathe war and long to be delivered from it, yet they are arming as never before for the next conflict, and are being driven by a power too great for them to resist. There can be no final deliverance from war until the hearts of men are changed, and the only sure hope is the Scriptural one of salvation for the individual and the race through the Lord Jesus Christ accepted as personal Savior, and crowned as king. His coming to reign as the prince of peace is the believers' remedy for the curse of war; and the sinful condition of the human heart, utterly unchanged as it is by any advances of science and evolution of civilization, makes this remedy the only one. Thank God, it is proved and sure.

The nominal churches of Christendom today prove by a thousand utterances and actions everywhere what they feel ought to be the attitude [of] the church of Jesus Christ towards war. Their duty to support the League of Nations and similar movements is instilled into their members as a necessary and logical part of practical Christianity. There is an admitted and instinctive feeling that opposition to the war spirit is the only possible attitude consistent with the spirt and teaching of Jesus Christ. Particularly noteworthy is the resolution of the 1930 Lambeth Conference—and a state church, such as the Church of England, is of necessity even more guarded in its declarations on such a subject than are other communions. It runs as follows: "When nations have solemnly bound themselves by treaty, covenant, and pact for the pacific settlement of international disputes, the conferences holds that the Christian church of every nation should refuse to countenance any war in regard to which the government of its own country has not declared its willingness to submit the matter in dispute to arbitration or conciliation."

Yet we feel reluctantly compelled to affirm that the churches as a whole miserably failed in the last, as in almost every preceding war in this matter of a firm and united stand against militarism. Patriotism surged over everything: its virtues were represented as the truest expression of the Christian life, and its sacrifices were upheld as evidencing the very spirit of Calvary. Different sections of the church, resident in different nations fighting each other to the death, invoked the blessing of God upon contending causes, and upon the most hellish means which those causes could devise to bring victory. Some churches became little better than recruiting stations.

It is little wonder that the utter farce and the tragic inconsistency of the whole business provoked the sneers and mistrust of a world grappling with fearful realities. As a relative of the writer said at the time, "It seems as if the churches have put their Christianity in the cupboard, to bring it out again after the war!" They have brought it out; and it is any wonder that it provokes very little enthusiasm? Right here, we suggest, is one of the main reasons for the indifference of this generation to the churches as a whole. In the hour of test they did not ring true enough to the spirit and teaching of their Founder. No wonder that any American daily somewhat cynically says, referring to the decision of the Lambeth Conference quoted above, "Great Britain's next war may be sprinkled with holy water like all the others." The attitude of the churches in the last war was little short of a tragedy. And in stating this we do not fail to appreciate the magnificent personal work of chaplains and many others, who, groping in the fog of inconsistency all around them, ministered as faithfully as they knew how to the spiritual needs of their fellows, and thus earned a well-merited personal respect.

It is probably safe to say that, however passionately patriotism may overwhelm everything else in time of war, the world certainly expects the Christian church to take a stand against war, and it is deeply disappointed at heart when that stand is not taken, however much it may persecute for the time the "conscientious objector."

"What Saith the Scriptures?"

This is the very heart of the question for the true disciple of the Lord Jesus Christ. The "Pentecostal" believer, above all others, will insist upon a Scriptural basis for whatever stand he may take. The consideration of the Bible on this matter will most readily suggest itself under the three heads.

The Old Testament

Immediately we find war of the bloodiest kind, wars of extermination, engaged in by God's chosen people, at God's express command, and with God's special blessing. Joshua 8; 1 Samuel 15; 2 Sam 5:24; etc. This seems in strange contradiction to the teaching of the New Testament at first sight. A moment's consideration will make us remember, however, that the divine government differs with the progressing dispensations, and the Old

"War, the Bible, and the Christian" [Part 1]

Testament is never the ultimate ground for the Christian to base his actions upon. Its history comprises "times of ignorance" at which God winked (Acts 17:30): its spiritual dynamic was a law written upon tables of stone, and enforced by heavy physical penalties on every hand (e.g., Leviticus 26, etc.); the very bringing in with Christ of a New covenant of which the keynote is the word "better" (Heb 8:6, etc.) was a proof of its temporary character. The chosen nation of Israel was the divine instrument of the law of righteousness to execute a well-merited judgment upon the iniquity of nations which had become "full" (Gen 15:16).

Before any parallel position can be claimed for modern nations engaging in ordinary warfare, such nations must produce evidence that they are in the same position towards God and the other nations as was Israel of old; which is manifestly impossible. It would be exceedingly difficult for Britain or Germany, France or the United States, or any other nation to justify any claim to the express command and blessing of God, after such claims are made in time of war by contending armies. Unfortunately, either pride or prejudice color the viewpoint far too much, and patriotism runs riot over everything.

The fact that Israelites of old went to war with the divine approval affords no basis for the Christian expecting the same if he participates in the wars of his country.

The Teaching of Jesus Christ

In the teaching and example of Jesus Christ the disciple finds his absolute ground for faith and practice. "Follow Me," rings out the Master, so clearly that none can fail to hear the call if they own His name.

The teaching of Jesus is almost too familiar to need restating. Such passages of Matt 5:21–48 are classical; all through He consistently teaches forgiveness of enemies and the suffering of wrong to the point of utter foolishness in the eyes of the world. His example is, if anything, even more striking. He makes no attempt at self-defense at any time, and in the Garden even insists upon nullifying the one act with a sword that was raised on His behalf. Moreover, He accompanies the act of healing with a pungent word on the very subject we are considering (Matt 26:51, 52). In all things "He was led as a lamb to the slaughter."

It is commonly admitted that the attitude of Jesus Christ towards war left no uncertainty. To quote a recent worldly periodical: "No Christian nation has ever taken seriously the clear and unequivocal teaching of the gospel on this subject. At the same time no Christian artist has ever represented the Galilean as commanding a machine-gun battalion or piloting a bombing plane." It has never been done simply because it is unthinkable. Yet Christians are called to be like Christ![1]

---

1. Gee, "War, the Bible, and the Christian" [Part 1], 6–7.

34

"War, the Bible, and the Christian" [Part 2]

Donald Gee

1930

The New Testament Church

AS TO THEIR ATTITUDE on war, the Acts and the Epistles carry on the same teaching and the same example as that recorded of Jesus. Acts 7:60; Rom 12:20; 1 Thess 5:15; Eph 4:32; etc. Forgiveness and the suffering of injury even (1 Cor 6:7) is the keynote right through. There is plenty of conflict, it is true, and military metaphors are freely used, but the warfare is strictly spiritual, and the weapons are "not carnal" (2 Cor 10:4). The foes which the Christian has to meet and overcome are those very spiritual forces of evil, and those very sins and passions which are most of all let loose in times of warfare, and which the active participant can hardly avoid sharing in.

Certain questions may be raised, however, which demand a fair inquiry. For instance, it may be argued that if the military profession is so opposed to Christian principles, then why did our Lord heal the soldier's servant? Why did the Holy Spirit fall upon Cornelius? Why has God blessed Christian soldiers, such as General Gordon and many others, right through the centuries?

The answer is, of course, that God meets us in grace during this dispensation, and demands of a soul only that it walk in all the light He has given it. There is no real question raised at all because Christ healed the centurion's servant, for He was "the friend of publicans and sinners," and He healed them all. In the case of the devout man Cornelius, it is plain that he was walking in all the light he possessed. One of the common fallacies among us is that divine blessing represents divine approval upon all that we are and all that we do. This does not follow, however, in this day of grace. The final explanation is that divine mercy is granted to us for Christ's sake, and not because of works of righteousness which we have done.

Moreover, the inspired teaching of the apostle was that conversion should disorganize as little as possible the social structure of the age in which they were living. "Let every man abide in the same calling wherein he was called" (1 Cor 7:20, etc.). The spiritual freedom which the slave found in Christ was of far more importance than his social liberty. This did not imply that the gospel endorsed slavery; its principles are diametrically opposed to it; and eventually the gospel triumphed, and wherever its light shone, slavery became gradually abolished. The same rule will apply to soldering. Where the Christian soldier had honorable obligations to fulfill, entered into before his conversion, we cannot imagine the apostle giving any other counsel that that given to the salve, "Abide in your calling," meanwhile, until a legitimate opportunity is afforded for freedom. This does not endorse militarism any more than 1 Corinthians 7 endorses slavery. There have doubtless been many men in military service who have never seen, or only dimly realized, how opposed such an occupation with all it involves must ever be to the spirit and teaching of Jesus Christ. God will bless such up to the light they have, if they do not play traitor to their own consciences but are sincerely "walking in the light" as far as they have it.

Having referred to "honorable obligations," we are now brought face to face with the most delicate and crucial issue of the whole question. This is to determine what shall be the attitude of a Christian when the very State to which he is commanded in the word of God to be in subjection "for conscience' sake" (Rom. 13:5) demands that he shall take up arms. This was the exact dilemma which multitudes of believers in the belligerent nations on both sides of the last war had to meet; which many are meeting right now in the countries where conscription is in force; and which all of us, at any time, may be called upon to meet again.

The Practical Application

It cannot be stated too emphatically that it is the duty of the Christian to be in subjection to the powers that be (Rom 13:1–8, etc.). They are "ordained of God." That is to say, God is always on the side of order and government, and always opposed to anarchy and lawlessness. The Christian's submission to

"War, the Bible, and the Christian" [Part 2]

the powers that be must always rise above mere shades of political opinion: he must be equally loyal to whatever political party may be in office. Mere personal disagreement with certain laws can never justify a Christian in disobeying or evading them; he should "for conscience' sake" scrupulously obey the slightest police order or by-law of the local magistrates and all the law of the land in which he dwells. Absolute loyalty to the State must be declared and actual policy of any section of the Christian church that aims at the approval of God. "Render unto Caesar the things that are Caesar's."

This may seem to settle the question once and for all, and apparently to leave no alternative for the Christian when the State commands but to obey. It should be remembered, however, that although God is on the side of order and government as opposed to anarchy and lawlessness, yet the men who comprise the governments of this world may often be sinners who have "no fear of God before their eyes"; or, at the best, are men compassed about by the infirmities shared by the whole human race. A situation may therefore arise at any time when a human government legislates along a line directly opposed to the revealed will of God contained in the Scriptures. This is a very different matter to a mere question of diversity of politics. When the clash is between the law of God and the law of man, then the only answer for the Christian is contained in the immortal words of Peter, "We ought to obey God rather than men" (Acts 5:29). Conscientious objection then becomes the only possible course, however serious the consequences. The Bible puts clear before us the magnificent example of Daniel and the three Hebrews (Daniel 3 and 6). He who said, "Render unto Caesar the things that are Caesar's" also said, "But unto God the things that are God's." The two are to be combined to the last possible limit, but when further combination of allegiance becomes impossible—then God must come first.

The Christian's true citizenship is in heaven (Phil 3:20, R.V.). He obeys the law of his earthly country in exactly the same way as an alien passing through. His ultimate allegiance is always to his heavenly King.

Patriotism is unfortunately allowed to run wild in so many believers. Even in times of peace narrow nationalistic prejudices are allowed to interfere with Christian fellowship. The writer remembers a convention in Scotland some years ago when objection was taken to speakers who on that occasion happened to be English! In the same way one sometimes finds prejudice of British against American preachers, and American against British preachers; and other such nationalistic feelings, all over the world. We fear that a perverted patriotism is far more deeply rooted in most of our hearts than becometh citizens of the heavenly kingdom of our Lord Jesus Christ; and if we are not careful it can make us very traitors to the true body of Christ. We are "all one" in Him.

Yet if patriotism can affect many so strongly in time of peace, is it any wonder that they are completely swept off their feet by its surging currents in time of war? Patriotism may have some legitimate and admirable means of outflow and expression—we do not suggest that we need to be entirely without it—but it requires deep personal crucifixion, and especially when it destroys Christian fellowship between brethren. More than all else we must be delivered from that unthinking patriotism which says, "My country, right or wrong."

The writer has observed as a solemn fact that those of our Pentecostal brethren who took a strongly patriotic attitude in the last war have mostly gone backward in spiritual power and influence ever since, while those who put Christ and His Word before all have advanced by divine grace to positions of spiritual leadership. It could hardly be otherwise.

The extent to which a believer feels called to maintain a conscientious objection to military service must always remain a personal matter. Many will feel that they have gone quite far enough in refusing to actually take life, and such will willingly take Red Cross work, or other non-combatant service. Others will feel that they cannot participate in definitely military service of any description; but are ready to undertake any work of national importance in a time of national crisis, such as farming or help in essential public services. Extremists may go even further, but it should be remembered that in the highly organized condition of modern society it is practically impossible to live in a State without participating in some way or other in its activities. Every individual must settle it between his own conscience and God.

The question of self-defense may arise in some minds. This was a favorite test-question in tribunals during the last war. The writer was asked, for instance, "What would you do if German soldiers were attacking your home, and on the point of killing your wife and children?" None of us dare state dogmatically what we would do under such circumstances; human instincts are very strong. But there is not much doubt as to what the Christian ought to do, even in such a position as that, to show forth the spirit of his Master. Peter used a sword in defense of Christ, but our Lord instantly repudiated his action and healed the slashed ear. Luke 22:51. Some wives would not ask for defense at such a time. One feels that there ought to be a

"War, the Bible, and the Christian" [Part 2]

trust in God to deliver, or else a suffering or whatever His will permitted. Calvary does not point at all in the direction of self-defense, and the appeal to the natural brute instincts which such a question entails can hardly have first place with a Spirit-filled child of God.

There is a justifiable fear on the part of the State and the public that "conscientious objection" may be used as a cloak for cowardice and mere shirking. This being so, the believer can hardly complain if his treatment is somewhat hard. Indeed, he will willingly submit to any fair test that can prove the genuineness of his conviction. And it was the writer's general experience that sincerity, once proved, won the respect even of those who could not agree altogether with the stand taken.

There can be no doubt whatever of the ultimate result, if Christians all over the world refused to participate in war and bloodshed. Even the New York Times, in referring to the Lambeth Conference Resolution quoted above, says, "If this were lived up to by all the members of that particular church around the globe, and they were joined by all the members of the other Christian churches, the end of war would be assured. The moral and economic sanctions against it would drive it at least beyond the borders of Christendom." These are words well worth pondering.

Much as love for poor war-weary humanity may make us long for such an issue, however, we believe that the true motive for the believer is not to be found even there; it is to be found in personal loyalty to our Saviour and King, and in a detestation of war and all it involves, because it is so absolutely opposed to His Spirit who has come to dwell in our hearts.

Los Angeles, Calif.[1]

---

1. Gee, "War, the Bible, and the Christian" [Part 2], 2–3.

35

"War Behind the Smoke Screen"

Pentecostal Evangel

1930

IN THIS BOOK [WAR behind the Smoke Screen] the Christian sees war, not only in its reality and grim awfulness, but in its true contrast to the teachings of Jesus Christ, as the writer lifts the veil of censorship, propaganda, and deceit, and shows his readers how extensive is the hold of darkness on the nations of the world.

Most readers will be amazed to discover how in the World War public opinion in regard to the war was molded by propaganda, and to see how the church failed in the hour of crisis. The reason why hundreds of thousands in the United States and millions in the rest of the world threw away their faith in God and their regard for the church becomes plain. Mr. Allen writes from first-hand knowledge received through extensive travels all over the world during and after the World War. He is a Christian who looks at the War and the future in the light of the gospel.

So severe and horrible was the war spirit in the United States even, that the New Testament was subjected to censorship because the teaching of Jesus regarding love for enemies and forgiveness were seen by military authorities to be contrary to their attempts to create the necessary hatred in the hearts of the people which would make them fighters. To quote Mr Allen:

"The Association to Abolish War, of Boston, Mass., when they desired to have the Sermon on the Mount printed for free distribution, without note or comment, were advised by federal authorities not to do so, on the ground that it might be considered pro-German. This happened during the winter of 1917–18. I elsewhere speak of the possibilities of "sedition" found in the Sermon on the Mount, in England, also during the Great War."

"War Behind the Smoke Screen"

What happened to those who, for conscience sake, refused to take up arms? Mr. Allen gives the reader a glimpse of the wide-spread reign of terror by which governments and war enthusiasts tried to force conscientious objectors to fight. We are amazed to find that the old Inquisition and its barbaric methods was with us again and that the public never knew what was going on behind the walls of censorship. Christians who expect to be true to the Lord in the coming days will find it necessary to check up on their consecration after reading what it means to oppose the powers of this world when they are dominated by hate and led by the destroyer.

Those of us who drift along unconcerned now that the sun shines, need to be jarred by this book. Those of us who have the great responsibility of influencing the thought and actions of others need to be informed of realities as they are, and to be awake to what it means to live in these days before the end. The reader is moved to exclaim with Paul, ". . . who is sufficient for these things?"

We have this book in stock at the Gospel Publishing House. The price is $1.50. Add 5 cents for postage.[1]

---

1. "War behind the Smoke Screen," 3. This is a book review about William Charles Allen's *War behind the Smoke Screen*. The Gospel Publishing House advertised this anti-war literature in *The Pentecostal Evangel*.

36

"The Way to Disarm Is to DISARM"
Aimee Semple McPherson
1932

Another armament conference is about to be held in Europe. The great powers are to decide how many guns each is to be allowed wherewith to kill the other.

There is something horrifying in this conference . . . shuffling and trickery as each nation tries—figuratively—to get the drop on the other—the one with naval stations trying to outwit the others with fewer naval stations.

Something is stupefying in the spectacle of great nations whose people have not a thing in the world against each other being taxed to the verge of starvation to build great military machines. And for what?

If the nations would stop building warships and equipping armies we would be all but overwhelmed with prosperity. The world would have more money and more happiness than at any time in history.

The pity and hideousness of it is that no one wants war. Not even the soldiers. Don't imagine for a minute that a gentle little shoemaker from Bavaria wanted to leave his family and go out to plunge a bayonet into the heart of the father of a little family in the grape vineyards of Normandy. They had to be goaded into it. Boys had to be poisoned with hatred, with tales of atrocities to make them fight. On that Christmas Day in No Man's Land between the trenches in France, the militarists had a shock. Homesick boys from Germany, England and France met in the shell-torn ground and exchanged presents and shook hands and would have ended the war then and there, but for the sudden tightening of discipline.

The nations all protest that they want peace; but they have to shout these protestations above the din of the cannon makers.

"The Way to Disarm Is to DISARM"
Civilization Will Die

The tortured, half-starved world cannot live through another war. The next will destroy civilization. The whole structure of modern civilization is in terrible danger. Anyone with common sense can see that. History shows that Aryan civilizations ordinarily last about fifteen hundred years. After that they sicken and die. They perish because they forsake the inexorable law.

The era of civilization that we call "our day" began in the darkness that followed the fall of Rome. That was just about fifteen hundred years ago. The implication is ghastly and terrible. The pity of it is that we are sinking when we could so easily save ourselves. We are going down in the bloodstained morass when all we need to do is follow the way.

Let us look at this problem with cold blooded, hard-boiled logic. Jesus Christ alone of all who have lived on this earth had complete wisdom. He knew the way. He tried to show us. For 2000 years, we have been trying to elude the simple and beautiful truth of His teaching. We have exercised every device of human ingenuity to do the stupid, the wicked and senseless way instead of the simple and true way. Diplomats have gabbled and dickered and dodged and intrigued and cheated and lied and deceived—and have brought the world to the brink of ruin. It would have been a happy world—and could be now—had they been willing to follow the simple doctrine of the Golden Rule. The Sermon on the Mount was the soundest diplomacy, the sanest business ethics, the most practical rule for success and happiness ever written or spoken in the whole history of the world.

He Said it All

Christ said it all. Those few, simple words contain the whole lesson of life. And that which He sated was the Inexorable Law. There is no way to get around it. It can't be tinkered with; or evaded or compromised. The Master gave the Law to the world in gentle, loving words—simple words that the smallest child could understand. But those words were final and inexorable.

Try to disobey that Law and see what you will get. Try to substitute hatred and double dealing and trickery for brotherly love and see where you will land. Big Business is already finding out. Throat cutting and driving competitors to wreck and ruin have had an alarming development. After bitterness and sorrow, bloodshed, tears and agony, it has been discovered that it is impossible to drive a competitor to ruin without going down in the wreck. In war, no nation can annihilate the other nation without suffering annihilation itself.

Oh, the sorrows and the tragedies that would have been saved to this poor old world had we but believed that Jesus Christ knew what He was talking about and meant what He said. This disarmament conference will result in nothing; they never do. One nation will slip over a sixteen-inch gun on a careless rival and will find that a new kind of poison gas has been slipped over in return. If civilization is to be saved, the world must cry "Stop"—and stop. The only way to disarm is to disarm.[1]

---

1. McPherson, "The Way to Disarm is to DISARM," 3.

37

"The Pulse of a Dying World"
William Booth-Clibborn
1933

Rabid Nationalism

JUST LIKE WITH THE individual "Pride goeth before destruction" (Prov 16:18) even so with the nations. If they are approaching the time of their final destruction, we may reasonably expect reckless blinding pride to lure them to their destined doom. Isaiah says that the Lord's Breath is "to sift the nations with the sieve of vanity" (Isa 30:28). This explains the present revival of fanatical nationalism.

Bridled Multitudes

Millions are being swept on to the vast catastrophe that must engulf civilizations. "There must be a bridle in the jaws of the people causing them to err" (Isa 30:28). The rising coercion of dictatorship is God's bridle in the mouth of the common masses. Individuality and personality, choice of action and freedom of thought, speech and press are ruthlessly stamped out as in Italy and Germany. The millions become mere automatons.

Oppressive Peace

The British tax, the heaviest, is $22.00 for every man, woman and child. Sir Robert Horne said of this intolerable burden, "We are painting the cart while starving the horse." The Western World staggers under the increasing oppression, solvent people so drained by taxes that the social services go unsupported, not to mention religion. The Nations in paying off public debts and spending millions on enormous armies and navies have turned peace into an oppression greater than war.

Germany Inflamed

Hitler's legions, 690,000 men, march all over Germany. The Reichswehr another 100,000 drill incessantly. The veterans clubs muster 800,000. The contagious enthusiasm of the Nazis inflames them all as Germany finds itself strangely stranded in the uncomfortable diplomatic isolation. Finding all doors closed Berlin may befriend the Bolshevists for her own ends. Expediency is often inconsistent. United to Russia she could repudiate her private debts (a fabulous sum) re-arm overnight and defy the world. "Blocked to the South we can smile on the North," shouted Adolf at Nuremberg.

Russia's Dilemna

While Germany talks war demanding an air-fleet, Russia concentrates all her efforts perfecting the greatest war machine in the annals of man; the whole populace is to be mobilized for the moment when Stalin decides that the only way out of the stupendous dilemma ten thousand soviet blunders have created—*is war*. Professors Zelle of Chicago and Salette of Berlin arrived in Finland prophesying the greatest famine in history impending. Twenty-million are doomed by this year's crop failures, the starving village peasants unearthed the seed potatoes and grain and secret cannibalism is reported widespread.

The Disarmament Dream

This cross-section of inflammatory tendencies, menaces and wars all over the earth shows the cause why the misled mass of Christian people double their efforts in checking the threatening holocaust of war. Nations in prophecy are Beasts and in reality worse. To pair their claws and blunt their fangs is risky disappointing business. The Methodists presented fifty million signatures and the Roman Catholic women twenty-five million petitioning the last Disarmament Conference to come to terms showing to what extent nominally Christian churches backed the movement. It meets this fall again foredoomed to failure as nationalism rises to fever heat in every country and the military spirit predominates.

Resist Not Evil (Matt 5:39)

Three forgotten words of Christ would revolutionize the whole of the apostate church's program. If, instead of spending mints of money in reform and using every means to coerce legislative bodies to adopt their viewpoint on social and moral questions, the church would return to the simple saving Gospel such a reviving would be the result as to solve its every problem. The church as a whole has lost its vision and is perishing as a consequence. When it loses faith in Calvary's message it will stoop to every form of social service and paralyze its spiritual usefulness. Instead of curing the disease of sin by divine power it bandages the wounds and applies them.

Preaching Prohibition

[Prohibition] is a case in point. With the steady march of the States voting for repeal of the Volstead Act, many prohibition prophets are proven false. The clergy are loath to leave liquor alone—the whole temperance question proved such a convenient practical issue—but now that repeal is assured what lady love shall they court? what message proclaim? "I cannot continue to preach prohibition and preach the gospel at the same time; the load is too heavy; so I am returning to my first love—preaching the Gospel," said Billy Sunday in Omaha recently. Sound advice—but after having prostituted preaching many will find it difficult to return to "the old paths" unless with thorough repentance. True wives resent lovemaking mates that have run after every mistress.

Sinning with the Sword

Apostate Christianity proudly struts about thinking itself the guardian of the spiritual and moral advances of civilization. That is why it abets and justifies carnal warfare for "righteous causes." All denominations as well as nations that have taken up the sword shall finally perish with it, for Christ did not only speak to the individual when addressing Peter in Gethsemane. Our Lord said, "For all they that take the sword shall perish with the sword"

(Matt 26:52). This word must have a larger fulfillment in the coming collapse. The fallen church has found pretext enough in every conflict to encourage the enlistment of its members; mistakenly appointed itself as the protector of the good it believes it has contributed to society. Failing to put up the sword in the last war it will draw it in the next!

Sanctified Slaughter

The words of Professor Hearing of Leyden University, Holland, are remarkable: "The manner in which the church in all Christian lands was directly involved in the mutual slaughter of the last War, as the indispensable, inspirational factor, demonstrates its fall in the clearest, cruellest way. No severer sentence can be passed on military Christianity of today than that which is passed by the Christianity of Christ. It has supplanted faith in the new creation with its own Creation belief, and has learned meekly to accept the world which Christ repudiated. Theology has contrived to reconcile the Christian to war, and provide militarism with that spiritual sanctification without which it could not last in the lands of the Christian confession." Everything true Christianity stands for is completely negated when Christians encourage and engage in war. The only fighting permitted the believer is that of Eph 6:12–18.

Conscientious Objectors

The mass of Church members being not converted it is to be expected that they will side with the world in the matter of war, and let no one prevent them becoming soldiers. They have never entered by new birth, the Kingdom of which Christ spoke when He said, "My Kingdom is not of this world: if my kingdom were of this world, then would my servants fight" (John 19:36). But the true, pure people of God throughout the centuries are those whose salting has affected the world most; they have never sought to legislate the nations into righteousness, nevertheless, their initiative and boldness in proclaiming the truth has inspired most of modern reforms and contributed greatly to the amelioration of human ills. Never discarding the Gospel, as the apostate church, they have insisted that it is the only adequate and certain means of regenerating the individual and through him improving conditions. Such Christians are true conscientious objectors.

"The Pulse of a Dying World"
Supreme Court Blunder

In a recent decision involving the application for citizenship of Dr. Macintosh with which 1500 other candidates were grouped, the United States Supreme Court denied those who could not, for conscientious reasons, subscribe to the oath of physically defending the country in the event of war, the privilege of becoming citizens. Six judges were equally divided but the supreme Evan Hughes cast the deciding negative vote. The whole State and Church question therefore looms up afresh in vicious form. The Nazis have grossly subordinated the German church. Italy preaches, "All in the state, nothing outside." In Russia the church is ground to powder and exterminated. In France conscripts are compelled to join the army or must languish in prison. Everywhere the State demands of the individual a fanatical, blind loyalty upon which he can place no limits. His conviction as to God's will is mocked and ignored. Each true Christian must prepare to face the issue afresh. "We ought to obey God rather than men" (Acts 5:29). The Supreme Court must answer before a greater and final Court of Appeal in Heaven for daring to put the State before God.[1]

---

1. Booth-Clibborn, "The Pulse of a Dying World," 12–13. Excerpt.

38

Is War Christian?
Frederic B. Phillips
1937

"By This . . . Know"

THAT WE ARE LIVING in an age when, generally speaking, the churches are getting emptied, and worldliness and pleasure seeking is on the increase, cannot be denied. The man in the street is fed up with religion, and very often points the finger of scorn at the churchgoer. He draws your attention to some shameful deed of a professing Christian, some shady deal of a deacon, or he sometimes says of the minister (God forbid, but I am afraid he is right in some cases) that he is only in the ministry for what he can make out of it.

Why is it, we ask, that things have got to this state? When Christ was on earth the multitudes thronged Him. They walked miles into the desert and went without food in order to hear the words of life which fell from His lips. Then when they were converted they gave up all, home, friends, business, yes and their lives too, in order to be true to Him who loved them.

Then what is the cause of this change? Has Christ changed? Emphatically, no! It is right to suppose that the man in the street is really opposed to true Christianity? Never! Let me quote Henry Drummond again; he says: "No man can ever be opposed to Christianity who knows what it really it. The working man would still follow Christ if He came among them. As a matter of fact they do follow anyone, preacher or layman, in pulpit or on platform, who is in the least like Him. But what they cannot follow and must evermore live outside of, is a worship which ends with the worshipper, a religion expressed only in ceremony, and a faith unrelated to life."

We have the answer to our question in the first sentence of the quotation just given. Let me repeat it—"No man can ever be opposed to

Christianity who knows what it really is." The trouble today is that men do not really know. The idea they have of Christianity is based on what they have seen and heard of it through professing Christians. Generally speaking this falls so short of what Christianity really is; for we professing Christians on every hand displaying anything but the spirit of Christ in their lives, not only towards the unsaved, but also to their own brothers and sisters in Christ. Can we expect men to receive the story of the love of Christ on Calvary, and believe the Sermon on the Mount which we preach, if by our actions we ourselves repudiate it all? I say, no, we cannot be surprised that the majority of men have an entirely wrong conception of what Christianity really is.

But worse than this, we all know how that during the Great War many of the clergy became recruiting agents, and I have been informed that war sermons were actually circulated to ministers. One of these was entitled "Salvation by Sacrifice," thus deliberately concealing its true meaning, which was nothing less than "Salvation by Murder."

Under such circumstances how can we expect men to know what real Christianity is? We cannot get away from the fact that they do not know, and the Church is undoubtedly suffering today as a result of her leaving the Gospel of peace and goodwill to take sides with the world and its armies of force. Then naturally we ask—How are men to know what real Christianity is? The answer comes from our Lord Himself—"By this shall all men know that ye are my disciples, if ye have love one to another" (John 13:35). Not love to God, mark you, but "love one to another." And I fail to see this love manifest when one man plunges a bayonet into another, or when one man shoots another, thus transforming a happy wife and family into a sorrowful widow and fatherless children.

There is no doubt that the man in the street cannot see any love in this any more than I can, and here you have the reason why many hundreds, no, thousands of men have not entered a church since the World War, except for a wedding or a funeral. If men know nothing else more about Christianity they do know that the Gospel of the Lord Jesus Christ is a gospel of peace on earth and goodwill toward men.

How long then will the Christian Church flounder on this question? For several centuries after Christ's death is was accepted without question that to be a Christian was to eschew war and all violence. Surely we all must agree that peace and goodwill lie at the very root of Christianity. It was Earl Haig himself who gave to the churches this unanswerable challenge: "It is your job to make my job unnecessary." Dr. F. W. Norwood, of the London City Temple, when he was instituted President of the National Free Church Council in April, 1935, said: "I see no alternative for the Churches but complete and final repudiation of war."

It is a calamity that the Church as a whole hesitates to proclaim fearlessly that as her Founder is the Prince of Peace so she must "follow after peace with all men," and whatever the consequences refuse to go hand in hand with the world in slaying precious souls for whom Christ died. Were the Church of Christ thus to stand loyal to her Master, the world would admire her instead of despising her; and the Church would by consistent life drive home to the conscience of the world its sinfulness.

The Church must take her stand in this way, otherwise men and women will turn elsewhere for help and guidance as indeed they are already doing, and the power of the Church will wane until her influence is almost entirely lost.[1]

War Versus Calvary

I want us to bring both war and Calvary together in our minds and view them side-by-side. Let us compare them.

In the first place we will all ask the question, In what way are they similar? I think the answer is, In one way only, and that is they both speak to us of the taking of life. In war we have the taking of thousands of lives, and mark you, without the slain having passed through any form of trial to ascertain whether they were guilty of death or not. At Calvary we have One only slain—the Lamb of God, our Savior. In war we have wholesale blood shedding. At Calvary we see the shed Blood. In war the object is rarely realized. On the other hand from Calvary we hear the triumphant words ring out: "It is finished," and we know that "He shall see of the travail of His soul and shall be satisfied."

Although one hears so much talk of sacrifice and laying down of one's life for King and country in wartime, I must remind you that this is not the object of war. On the contrary, the object of war is not only to take life, but to take as many lives as possible in as short a time as possible, with the least possible expense.

---

1. Phillips, *Is War Christian?*, 13–17. Excerpt.

How different is this from Calvary. It is written, "Christ came not to destroy men's lives, but to save." Then again we read, "While we were yet sinners (or enemies by wicked works) Christ died for us."

Hatred is the spirit of war, while love is the spirit of Calvary. It is this hatred shown in the hearts of the people by the reports of the wicked deeds of the enemy, that creates and stimulates the war fever. So this fever spreads until practically everybody does something, thus eventually gathering up sufficient force to conquer.

On the other hand, although it was force that seemingly conquered the meek and lowly Jesus when the soldiers nailed Him to the cross and one of them thrust that spear into His side, it was love, the greatest force on earth and in heaven, that gained the victory. Yes, the soldiers' seeming victory turned out to be defeat, but Christ's seeming defeat was the most glorious victory this old world has ever seen. It was victory for all time and eternity, for He broke the chains of sin which we could not; and now all who believe are "more than conquerors through Him that loved us."

We all must admit that the most glorious victory in war is terrible when we think of the thousands of young lives sacrificed, and the sorrow and suffering brought to thousands more. Especially is this so when we realize that the gain is only earthly and temporal. But the victory of Calvary is lovely to think of, and it fills hundreds of thousands the world over with an indescribable joy and peace. It causes joy among the angels in heaven, too.

Yes, Calvary was war indeed! But is was war between God and the Devil, and God won, Hallelujah to His Name. How did he win? Can we learn a lesson? I think we can. He won by love, real sacrificial love. This is how He won all through His life on earth. This is how He won in death. And listen, this is how He calls us to win. He says to His disciples, "Follow Me." Reader, will you follow Him in this way?[2]

Fluid Morals

Recently, when discussing this subject of whether a Christian should fight, a dear brother in Christ said to me that if I could give him a scripture which definitely stated that a Christian should not go to war then he would agree with me. He argued that although the scriptures teach us that it is absolutely wrong for an individual to kill in the ordinary course of life, yet to take life

2. Ibid., 29–32.

in war was an entirely different matter, and he contended that there was nothing in scripture to prove this to be wrong.

Strange reasoning this! Yes indeed, but it is worse than strange. It is dangerous, for it means that the whole code of morals is swept from under our feet. Then let us examine the logic of this argument closely, and see where it leads us.

Briefly it states that if any government goes to war then it is right for the people (Christian or otherwise) of that country to kill the common enemy, but apart from war it states that it is absolutely wrong to kill. In other words, supposing two ungodly rulers quarrel and go to war, then it becomes right to do what is wrong at any other time. Why? Because this ungodly ruler orders you do to it, of course!

Then let us imagine Britain is at war again with Germany, or France for that matter, it does not affect the argument whatever country it is. It becomes right, according to my friend's theory for the Christian in Britain to go to the front and kill the Germans or French, as the case may be. Let us take a flying trip to Germany. Imagine you were born there, and that you are an earnest Christian, for there are many earnest Christians in that country. Now it becomes right for you to go to the front and kill the British. Thus we would have Christians of one nationality fighting Christians of another nationality; in other words we would have a state of civil war in Christ's heavenly kingdom.

Do you see the folly of this reasoning? If it is right for one nation then it is right for another. Thus we are accusing God of fighting against Himself, and we know that "if a kingdom be divided against itself, that kingdom cannot stand."

But our friends will quote scripture. They will say it states in Romans 13 that we must obey our rulers... perhaps other scriptures will throw light on the subject. We will look at Acts 4:19–20: "But Peter and John answered and said unto them, Whether it be right in the sight of God to hearken unto you more than unto God, judge ye. For we cannot but speak the things which we have seen and heard."

You remember that they had been forbidden by the authorities to speak any more in the name of Jesus, and this was their reply.

Then in 1 Pet 2:13–15 we are told clearly that we are to submit for the Lord's sake.

Here is the passage: "Submit yourselves to every ordinance of man for the Lord's sake: whether it be to the king, as supreme; Or unto governors, as unto them that are sent by him for the punishment of evildoers, and for the praise of them that do well. For so is the will of God, that with well doing ye may put to silence the ignorance of foolish men."

Surely it is obvious to all my readers from the above that we, as Christians, are called upon by the Word of God to obey every law made by the authorities that does not entail disobedience to the Word of God. But when their orders or laws are directly opposed to the law of God, then obedience to God comes first.

Now let us return to my friend's theory. You will recall that he argued that in war it is right to kill the common enemy, but that in peace it is wrong to kill.

I may equally argue that in war it is also right to lie and to steal, to wound and be cruel, for these are necessary evils in the great machine of war. With regard to this I will quote the Rev H. R. L. Sheppard, C.H., D.D. In his book, *We Say No*, he writes:

> Right and wrong aren't fluid. The moral quality of an action doesn't depend on its results . . . The fact that I may gain a personal advantage by stealing doesn't make it morally right or me to do so. Even if I stole from people who wouldn't miss the money and handed over the proceeds of my crime to the unemployed, it still wouldn't be morally right . . . Still less could I justify killing a man, though I might think that the world would be a better place without him . . . Does it make any real difference to the moral quality of this action of killing if I put on a uniform to do it, and if the majority of my fellow-countrymen consider it praiseworthy? I can't honestly think it does. I have to answer to my conscience for what I do, and my conscience can't get beyond that injunction, "Thou shalt not kill."[3]

---

3. Ibid., 33–37.

39

"Conscientious Objection"
Donald Gee
1940

THOROUGHLY SINCERE CONSCIENTIOUS OBJECTION upon any subject usually wins the respect, if not the agreement, of all fair-minded people. Underlying a lot of popular contempt for the "conchie" is the assumption that he may be either a coward or a shirker. Due allowance must also be made for shallow thinking that sees only a method of escape from the universal toll of sacrifice and suffering that war imposes. We can sympathize with natural sentiment, even when we are its victims. Christians ought to be very thankful for a Government that provides legal recognition and exemption for proved conscientious objection to military service. Those who desire to avail themselves of the right of conscientious objection have both the legal and moral responsibility to establish the unquestionable sincerity of their claims, and the foundation upon which they are made. This is a serious matter for all parties concerned.

For our help towards clearer thinking and more consistent action at a time like this, the following hints are offered. They arise from actual conversations all over the country during recent weeks and months.

(1) It is palpably inconsistent to work upon armaments, making shells, bombs, aeroplanes, etc., and then object later to personal military service. Any Tribunal will quite logically refuse to see much conscientious distinction between using weapons myself, and making them for the other fellow to use. It may be argued that at a time like this the whole nation is more or less inevitably engaged in prosecuting the War; and this must be admitted. There are, however, inner and outer circles of connection with the actual war machine, and a conscientious objector should see to it that he keeps in the outermost circles. Forestry, the growing of food, the maintenance of essential public services, are the type of occupation that need involve

"Conscientious Objection"

no defilement of conscience. Not so, direct participation in the making of armaments, and the inconsistency is only aggravated if the armament work ensures drawing a generous salary.

(2) There ought to be some heart searching as to whether presumed conscientious objection does really spring from deep conviction, or only from an almost unrecognized desire to take any means of escape from the danger and discomfort of military service. Tribunals are quite fair when they ask an objector to produce evidence that proves his sincerity. "Actions speak louder than words." Have we manifested a tenderness of conscience in other matters besides military service? Have we ever voluntarily lost a job for conscience sake, because we felt it was not morally clean and involved the handling of goods, or the using of methods inconsistent with Christian principles? Have we ever proved by sacrificial action that we put first the Kingdom of God and his righteousness? Have the claims of the Lord's Day, and the Lord's service, been put before either personal ease or personal gain? These may be searching questions, but all will agree that there is something suspicious about a conscience that only comes to life when a war breaks out and military service is demanded.

Opportunity for previous proof of conscientious objection may not have occurred; but consistent Christian living should at least been manifested.

(3) We must be careful to distinguish between personal and political opinions and prejudices, and downright objection for conscience' sake because of Christian convictions. Do we simply disagree with this particular war? If so, then a Tribunal may justly affirm that our objection is political rather than religious, and judge us on that basis. One brother told me that he would have no objection to "having a smack at Russia" because of that nation's official godlessness!

The proper Christian conscientious objector disagrees with the whole business of war if he objects at all, and he ought to recognize that his principles apply equally whether the particular cause is considered to be wrong or right. He accepts the principle of Calvary, and the refusal to use physical force as a means to attain victory over evil. Such objection is based upon simple obedience to Jesus Christ, and an acceptance of them as the final rule for the disciple, whatever the cost.

At a time when political feeling is running high, and is fed by constant propaganda, the Christian needs to keep himself unspotted from the world in thought as well as deed. If we suffer, let us suffer as Christians, and not as meddlers in politics of the nations of the world.

(4) Conscientious objectors should avoid the fanatical. There are bound to be some extremists thrown to the surface at a time like this, and it may be the delight of some Tribunals to goad such on to make absurd statements that can give only offence to sober-minded people. Moffatt's translation of 1 Pet 3:15–16 is both beautiful and helpful in this connection: "Always be ready with a reply for anyone who calls you to account for the hope you cherish, but answer gently, and with a sense of reverence; see that you have a clean conscience, so that, for all their slander of you, these libellers of your good Christian behaviour may be ashamed."

It should be remembered that others may be compelled innocently to suffer for the fanaticism of those in whom the world recognizes no distinction.

(5) Conscientious objectors do well to make a special study of the book of Daniel, for the story of the three friends of Daniel, and then of Daniel himself, provide an inspired pattern. They were reasonable and considerate where the scruples and interests of others were concerned (Dan 1:12–13): their courage was superb in that their deliverance, even by divine intervention, was quite secondary to their loyalty to the dictates of conscience (Dan 3:17–19): they found a new and wonderful fellowship with God through their suffering for conscience sake (Dan 3:25): they were ready and willing to serve the very State that had persecuted them once their rights of conscience had been established. Dan 3:30. Daniel was the chief of the "presidents" over the Empire. Dan 6:2.

All of which is written for our instruction, and comfort. In conscientious objection we have need of a high order of moral courage, coupled with a sense of justice both for the State and for the objector. It is selfish to enjoy all the very real benefits of citizenship in a land which is the envy of less favored countries, and not to be prepared to give in return such loyal service as may be possible without compromise of Christian principle. Those with the highest motives may nevertheless be called to suffer, if they insist on personal loyalty to God as well as to Caesar, but they can rest assured that great spiritual enrichment lies in the path of the highest duty. Daniel became heaven's "Man, greatly beloved."

The pathway of suffering for Christ's sake carries with it the richest of all rewards. We may rest assured that the witness within of divine approval can be the portion of those with widely differing convictions as to what constitutes their personal path of duty. The purest conscientious objection carries with it the broadest tolerance for the sincere convictions of others, and finds its spiritual fellowship not in common agreement upon some creed, but in common loyalty to the truth as each one has found it in Christ.[1]

---

1. Gee, "Conscientious Objection," 4. This article, which appeared in "Redemption Tidings," although prepared for British readers, expresses the attitude of US Pentecostals in the matter of military service.

Bibliography

Backus, Elbert Carlton. "The Patriotic Harlot." *The Comeouter* (March 1, 1918) 4–7.
Bartleman, Frank. "Christian Citizenship." *Word and Witness* (1919/1920) 1–2.
———. "Christian Preparedness." *Word and Work* (1916) 114–15.
———. "The European War." *Weekly Evangel* (July 10, 1915) 3. From the collection of the Flower Pentecostal Heritage Center. Printed with permission from the Gospel Publishing House.
———. "In the Last Days." *Word and Work* (September 1916) 393–94.
———. "Is Christian Civilization Breaking Down?" *Christian Evangel* (February 27, 1915) 3. From the collection of the Flower Pentecostal Heritage Center. Printed with permission from the Gospel Publishing House.
———. "Present Day Conditions." *Weekly Evangel* (June 5, 1915) 3. From the collection of the Flower Pentecostal Heritage Center. Printed with permission from the Gospel Publishing House.
———. *War and the Christian.* n.p., after 1921.
———. "What Will the Harvest Be?" *Weekly Evangel* (August 7, 1915) 1–2. From the collection of the Flower Pentecostal Heritage Center. Printed with permission from the Gospel Publishing House.
———. "The World War." *Word and Work* (1916) 296–97.
"Blood against Blood." *Weekly Evangel* (July 3, 1915) 3. From the collection of the Flower Pentecostal Heritage Center. Printed with permission from the Gospel Publishing House.
Booth-Clibborn, Arthur Sydney. *Blood against Blood.* n.p., 1914.
Booth-Clibborn, Samuel. "The Christian and War: Christ Cleansing the Temple." *Weekly Evangel* (May 19, 1917) 4–5. From the collection of the Flower Pentecostal Heritage Center. Printed with permission from the Gospel Publishing House.
———. "The Christian and War: Is it Too Late?" *Weekly Evangel* (April 28, 1917) 5. From the collection of the Flower Pentecostal Heritage Center. Printed with permission from the Gospel Publishing House.
———. *Should a Christian Fight?* Swengel, PA: Bible Truth Depot, 1910?
Booth-Clibborn, William. "The Pulse of a Dying World." *The Latter Rain Evangel* 26, no. 1 (1933) 12–13.
Burgess, Stanley, and Eduard M. Van Der Mass. *International Dictionary of Pentecostal and Charismatic Movements.* Grand Rapids: Zondervan, 2003.

Bibliography

Frodsham, Stanley. "From the Pentecostal Viewpoint." *The Pentecostal Evangel* (June 21, 1924) 4–5. From the collection of the Flower Pentecostal Heritage Center. Printed with permission from the Gospel Publishing House.

———. "Our Heavenly Citizenship." *Word and Witness* (Septermber 11, 1915) 3.

Gee, Donald. "Conscientious Objection." *The Pentecostal Evangel* (May 4, 1940) 4.

———. "War, the Bible, and the Christian" [Part 1]. *The Pentecostal Evangel* (November 8, 1930) 6–7. From the collection of the Flower Pentecostal Heritage Center. Printed with permission from the Gospel Publishing House.

———. "War, the Bible, and the Christian" [Part 2]. *The Pentecostal Evangel* (November 15, 1930) 2–3. From the collection of the Flower Pentecostal Heritage Center. Printed with permission from the Gospel Publishing House.

Graves, Frederick A. "Red, White, and Blue." Hymn. November 16, 1901.

McCafferty, Burt. "Should Christians Go to War?" *The Christian Evangel* (January 16, 1915) 1. From the collection of the Flower Pentecostal Heritage Center. Printed with permission from the Gospel Publishing House.

McPherson, Aimee Semple. "The Way to Disarm Is to DISARM." *Los Angeles Times*, February 1932, J3.

Parham, Charles. "Everlasting Gospel." Sermon preached in Zion City, Illinois, August 27, 1914. Text: Jer. 16:4.

———. "War! War! War!" In *Everlasting Gospel*. 1911. Reprint n.p., n.d.

"The Pentecostal Movement and the Conscription Law." *Weekly Evangel* (August 4, 1917) 6.

"Pentecostal Saints Opposed to War." *Weekly Evangel* (June 19, 1915) 1. From the collection of the Flower Pentecostal Heritage Center. Printed with permission from the Gospel Publishing House.

Phillips, Frederic B. *Is War Christian?* London: Victory 1937.

Pipkin, Brian, and Jay Beaman. *Pentecostal and Holiness Statements on War and Peace*. Eugene, OR: Pickwick, 2013.

Reade, H. Musgrave. "The Spirit of the Age." *Trust* (November 1917) 13–5.

Seymour, William J. *The Doctrines and Discipline of Azusa Street Apostolic Faith Mission by William J. Seymour*. Complete Azusa Street Library 7. Joplin, MO: Christian Life, 2000.

Thistlethwaite, Lillian. "Victory." Apostolic Faith 1, no. 4 (June 1912) 1–3.

Tomlinson, A. J. "Days of Perplexity." *Church of God Evangel* (January 26, 1918) 1.

———. "Loyalty and Perseverance." *Church of God Evangel* (October 21, 1916) 1, 4.

———. "The Awful War Seems Near." *Church of God Evangel* (March 31, 1917) 1.

———. "The Awful World War." *Church of God Evangel* (February 24, 1917) 1.

———. "The Present Situation." *Church of God Evangel* (March 6, 1915) 1.

———. "War Notice." *Church of God Evangel* (August 4, 1917) 3.

"War behind the Smoke Screen." *The Pentecostal Evangel* (December 6, 1930) 3.

Subject Index

(the) 2% who profit vs the 98% poor, 62

affirm rather than swear, 92
Albigenses, 23
American Indian genocide, 56
anarchy, 2, 8, 138, 139
Anglo-Boer War, 21
Anti-Semitism, 120
Anti-Semitism and WWI, 118
apostasy, 12, 13, 14, 23, 79, 103, 105, 108, 117, 124, 149-150
approved occupations for Christians in wartime; forestry, agriculture, public service, 158
arms manufacture occupation disapproved, 158, 159

capital punishment, 99
capitalism, 51, 52, 54, 105
capitalism; greed critiqued, 2, 40, 41, 44, 45, 54, 55, 56, 61, 62, 65, 66, 119, 120
carnal weapons; war, 24, 25, 28, 29, 43, 73, 85, 87, 107, 108, 116, 117, 124, 137, 149
chivalry; honor; duty critiqued, 7, 22, 62, 84, 85, 89, 101, 133, 154, 155
Christendom critiqued, 19, 36, 42, 43, 47, 48, 49, 52, 81, 115
Christians must disobey government at times, 11, 67, 68, 99, 108, 109, 110, 111, 121, 139, 151, 156, 6, 27, 29, 57, 58, 83, 84, 86, 105, 106, 108, 122, 123, 139

citizenship in heaven, 140
civil religion, 78
cleansing the temple (Jesus' use of force), 72
COGIC; Church of God in Christ, 95
come out, 24
concentration camps, 21
conscientious objection, 14, 95, 115, 116, 118, 134, 139, 140, 141, 143, 150, 158, 159, 160, 161
conscientious objector training, 90, 91
conscientious objector; persecuted by Pentecostal and Holiness members, 119
conscientious objector; too late to join church to become CO, 92
Constantine, 23
contradiction human progress in destroying civilization, 37, 64
contradiction love and hate, 7, 153
contradiction; Christians killing Christians, 7, 44
contradiction; individual killing is wrong, killing in war is right, 155
contradiction; pray for and kill another human, 6
contradiction; pray for peace, pray for victory in war, 103
contradiction; praying for peace, while profiting from war, 34
Crusades, 23, 120

Subject Index

D.D.'s (Doctor of Divinity) renamed dumb dogs who cannot bark. Afraid of being prophetic and speaking against war, 121
Daniel and Revelation, 7, 39
Daniel of Babylonian captivity as example of conscience, 8, 14, 68, 110, 160
death in battle as passport to heaven, 78, 112, 113
democracy, 56
disarmament, 144
dispensation, 25, 44, 70, 73, 74, 106, 121, 134, 137
draft counseling, 92
draft counseling by Donald Gee (implied), 158
"drone" ship, 119
Drummond, Henry, 152

early church rejection of bearing arms, 115
early church; peace teaching and example, 23, 43, 106, 109, 110, 115, 123, 130, 130
England critiqued, 52, 53, 54, 55, 64

family institution destroyed by war, 37, 40
flags, 15, 16, 23, 24, 34, 65, 102, 102, 111, 113, 114
follow Jesus, 135
forgive, 17, 102, 111, 135, 137, 142
Free Church Council, England, 154
free press, 14
free speech, 14

genocide; American Indian, 56
Germany lauded, 53, 55
greed, 34

harlot, 101, 103, 104, 105, 123, 124
hell literalized, war spiritualized (spiritual warfare), 84
holy war critiqued, 42, 51, 103, 118
horses, slaughter of, 65
human progress, 37, 60, 61, 80
hypocrisy, 34

idolatry, 8, 13, 15, 15, 16, 78, 79, 81, 102, 103
inequality; rich getting richer, poor getting poorer, 65
inflation, 65
Inquisition, 23, 116, 143
interwar pacifism critiqued, 134, 154

Jesus' example of nonresistance, 9, 57, 59, 69, 72, 83, 87, 108, 111, 123, 124, 135, 155
Jesus' teaching nonresistance, 4, 19, 29, 43, 49, 70, 83, 86, 87, 93, 94, 95, 117, 119, 121, 129, 133, 135, 138, 142, 146, 153, 159
judgment of nations, 34, 35, 35, 36, 39, 41, 42, 45, 53, 58, 60, 147
Just War theory (implicit) violated, 119

lamb lay down beside the wolf (reversed), 23
Lambeth Conference, 1930; pacifism in British established churches, 133
Leavenworth Prison, xix, 116
love your enemies, 17, 94, 120, 129, 142
loyalty limited, 57, 67, 94, 139, 151
loyalty to God, 19, 25, 57, 67, 68, 68, 160, 161
loyalty to Jesus, 92
Lusitania, 41

Making the world safe for democracy, 14
mammon; god of hate and murder, 6
mark of the beast in buying and selling, 98
Mason, Charles H., 95
Mauro, Philip, 13
Mennonites, 11
mental illness increased by war stress, 61
Methodists, 11, 102, 103, 104, 148
Moloch, 8, 19, 119
moral hazard, 121
moral hazard for soldiers, 122
Moravians, 23
munitions profits, 45, 52, 62
murder of the innocents, 36, 65

Subject Index

nationalism, 3, 4, 7, 10, 11, 17, 37, 40, 45, 47, 49, 52, 58, 60, 78, 78, 79, 81, 81, 111, 139, 147, 149, 156
new theologies, 20
no time for carnal war (too busy), only time for work of gospel (spiritual war), 84
noncombatant Pentecostals drafted, 50, 3, 10, 17, 17, 70, 71, 91, 93, 94, 108, 109, 149
non-resistance directly related to religious reform, 103
Norwood, F. W., 154

obey Christ's laws, 68
obey government in all that does not conflict with laws of Christ, 68
Old Testament wars, 70, 134
Origen, 130

pacifism (e.g. political pacifism critiqued), 12, 69, 124, 130, 134
patriotism, 3, 4, 8, 9, 11, 12, 13, 14, 15, 19, 33, 36, 37, 44, 54, 67, 71, 78, 79, 84, 86, 88, 89, 101, 102, 103, 110, 112, 113, 119, 120, 123, 124, 133, 134, 135, 139, 140, 163
Pentecostals failed in following Jesus against war, 122
Peterson, Paul; REEM, suffered WWI; reaffirmed Pentecostal pacifism in Germany, 116
Pilgrims, 110, 116, 124
political pacifists in US 1915–1916 out-performed Christians in resistance, 69
Pope, critiqued, 34, 36, 52, 78
propaganda, 78, 122

Quakers, 11, 15, 50, 93, 115, 128

reconcile, 17

removal from membership for war service, 92
right to assemble, 14
rise and fall of nations, 2, 3, 7, 8, 42

Salvation Army, Salvationists, 11
second generation non-resistance, 132
separation from the world, 14, 24, 29, 57, 106
Sermon on the Mount, 93, 121, 129, 142, 145, 153
Sheppard, H. R. L., Rev., *We Say No*, 157
socialism, 2
socialism criticized, 12, 24, 35, 69, 105
socialist, 120
spies in all Pentecostal meetings, 120
Spiritual Kingdom, 27
sympathy is being lost, 61

Tertullian, non-resistant, 115

vegetarian, 64
veterans increase crime rates, 114

Waldenses, 23
war as a spiritual power, 20, 133, 137
war as a spiritual power (Antichrist), 15, 32, 79, 105, 106, 107, 109, 110, 111, 113, 124, 125
war as efficient killing (e.g. technological progress), 118, 154
war hymn, Onward Christian Soldiers, 120
war hymn, sung in Pentecostal meeting in London, 118
war hymns rewritten as antiwar songs, 1
war sends souls to hell, 32
war sermons (pro-war), 153
war to end war, 79, 133
Wesley, John, 106
WWI is uncivilized, 31
WWI is unjust war, 31
WWJD; what would Jesus do?, 87

Scripture Index

Genesis
12:1	70
15:16	135

Exodus
20	15, 94

Leviticus
17:8	70
17:9	70
18:21	119
26	135

Deuteronomy
7:1	70
27:15	13

Joshua
8	134

1 Samuel
15	134

2 Samuel
5:24	134

Psalms
45:10	89
50:22	60
69:9	74
91:1	85
120:7	131
149:4–9	58

Proverbs
3:5, 7	32

Song of Solomon
1:5, 6	89

Scripture Index

Isaiah

3:2	40
4:1	40
6:1	89
26:9	62
30:28	147
45:22	13
58:8–11	29
63:9	29

Jeremiah

3:9	13
12:5	121

Daniel

1:12–13	160
3	71, 139, 160
4:26	58
6	13, 160
9:23	68, 70, 71, 83, 87, 94, 95, 108, 135
10:11, 19	68, 70, 71, 83, 87, 94, 95, 108, 135

Matthew

5	49
6	6, 83
18:20	70
21:12	72
22:17–22	7, 27
23:38	75
24:12–13	63
26:51–52	28, 29, 135, 150

Mark

11:15–18	72, 73
12:15–16	98

Luke

2:14	94
6:46	67, 68
11:2–32	98
12:11–12	87
19:45	72
21:28	125
22:35–38	29
22:49–51	28, 140

John

2:13	72
2:17	74
2:19	72
8:9	73
13:35	7, 153
15:18,19	8, 9, 15, 106
15:20	11
17:16	29, 83, 84, 86
18	83, 86
19	150

Acts

4	11, 67, 156
5:29	139, 151
5:41	110
7:60	137
17:26–30	60, 135

Scripture Index

Romans

12:17–21	10, 17, 71
12	17, 95, 97, 137
13	8, 10, 110, 138

1 Corinthians

3:16–19	32, 75
4:13	14
5	86, 112
6:7	137
7:20	138
8:23	15
9:21	27
10:26	14
13	100

2 Corinthians

2:4	32
5:20	105
4:4	12
10	29, 137

Galatians

1:4	14, 57
6:10	108
6:14	15, 57

Ephesians

4:22, 32	95, 137
6:11–18	29, 150

Philippians

3:20	6, 29, 70, 84, 86, 105, 139

Colossians

1:13	57, 106
3:3	85

1 Thessalonians

1:9	15
5	29, 95, 112, 137

1 Timothy

2:1–4	82, 86

2 Timothy

2:7–8	32, 109

Hebrews

4:12	29
8:6	135
10:30	95
12	94, 95
13:13	69

James

1:27	29
4:1	109, 130
4:4	15
5	41, 62, 125

1 Peter

1:21	87
2	27, 57, 74, 156
3:15–16	160
4:17	117

2 Peter

3:11, 12	43

1 John

2:15	15
3:17–18	29
4:3	15

Revelation

6	52, 121
7:14–17	71
11:15	14, 109
13	14, 15, 95, 107
17:16–17	105, 124
18	52
19:11–21	58

www.ingramcontent.com/pod-product-compliance
Lightning Source LLC
Chambersburg PA
CBHW051744230426
43670CB00012B/2149